ASCENDING THE MOUNTAIN

Edited by Eltin Griffin, O Carm

Ascending the Mountain: The Carmelite Rule Today

PAPERS FROM THE O CARM/OCD CONFERENCE
ON THE RULE OF ALBERT
HELD AT DALGAN PARK, AUGUST 2002

First published in 2004 by
the columba press
55A Spruce Avenue, Stillorgan Industrial Park,
Blackrock, Co Dublin

Cover by Bill Bolger
Origination by The Columba Press
Printed in Ireland by ColourBooks Ltd, Dublin

ISBN 1 85607 449 8

Acknowledgements
Scripture quotations are from the New Revised Standard Version, copyright © 1989, by the Division of Christian Education of the National Council of the Churches of Christ in the United States of America. Used by permission.

Table of Contents

WORKSHOPS

Preface

The conference on the *Rule* of St Albert of Jerusalem held at Dalgan Park outside Dublin in August 2002 was an important event. Some of its papers were by those of scholarly competence and give insights and information not hitherto accessible in English. All the contributors, however, were experts, people of lived experience of the Carmelite *Rule,* either as enclosed nuns or more active friars. Their reflections are a serious contribution to the task of re-interpreting the *Rule* for our time. This is a challenge not only for nuns and friars, but for many others in the Carmelite Family, as well as for all who have found distilled wisdom for their lives in this ancient *Rule.*

This book also contains notes from the highly successful workshops. By their nature workshops cannot be adequately recorded: each is an event, a happening arising out of shared experience and reflection. People bring their gifts and insights to a workshop; they take from the workshop what they find inspirational for their own lives. The workshop notes here cannot do justice to the richer dynamic of open, shared experience. But they can still offer thoughts, insights, questions and perhaps inspiration for those who read this book.

I am grateful for all the co-operation which made the publication of this little volume possible. The idea of this conference came from the OCD Nuns' Association, who chose the *Rule* as a topic for on-going formation and invited the Friars on board. I thank especially the provincials, O Carm and OCD, our nuns and friars and the Tallow community which produced the work. Lastly, we all owe a debt of gratitude to the contributors and especially to those who attended the conference and in some cases invited the authors to refine their thoughts.

Eltin Griffin, O Carm
17 September, 2003
Feast of St Albert of Jerusalem.

Introducing the Conference

Eltin Griffin O Carm

It is indeed a privilege for me to have been invited to inaugurate this unique event, and to introduce the different speakers and various sessions each day.

The *Rule* reminds us that we all come out of the same stable. We have developed our different traditions across the years, but all the different traditions emanate from the same root and from a common trunk. Traditions vary not only among the O Carms and OCDs, but as I have discovered, within individual provinces of the friars one encounters very differing traditions.

We have come together on previous occasions over the past decade. The representatives of our Provincial Councils have met annually. The nuns have got so accustomed to coming together that they now take such meetings for granted. The friars in more recent times have shared in the Pilgrimage to Knock on the last Sunday of July each year.

Our various comings together reached a high point in the Millennium Year 2000. The highlight of that year was Leighlinbridge, which commemorated the arrival of the Carmelites in Ireland in 1271. Friars, nuns and laity assembled in the Town Park beside the River Barrow in beautiful weather on 20 September to hear our story retold by a local historian, erect a monument and to plant an oak tree, both very visible in that lovely setting.

The first meeting of the two General Councils took place on 6 December 1991. It was decided then to hold two meetings a year: in May in the O Carm Curia, and in December in the OCD Curia.

But then came an event which exceeded all our expectations, the visit of the Relics of St Thérèse of Lisieux in 2001 from 15 April into early July. As a result "Carmelite" became a household word overnight. Thérèse enabled us to work together in a project, which drew only positive reactions from the media.

To return to the business of the days ahead, the Carmelite *Rule.*

With the renewal of religious life as proposed by Vatican II, the various orders and congregations in the church have gone back to the foundations documents. There has been a huge body of writing, for instance, on the *Rule* of St Benedict by both men and women writers, monastic and lay. Much research has been done on the *Rule* of Augustine shared not only by the Augustinian family, but by a whole host of other orders and congregations, including the Dominicans. The *Rule* of St Francis and the foundation writings of the Franciscan family have given new life to those who follow in the footsteps of the Poverello. The family of Francis is almost like a church within a church.

Our Carmelite *Rule* has occasioned a number of Congresses from the 70s to the 90s: Sassone in 1970; Niagara Falls in 1987; Texas in 2000 and now in Ireland at Dalgan Park. We have not been able to muster as many friars as we would like . The OCDs are suffering from the "fall out" following their Chapter. For the O Carms, schools and chaplaincies re-open this week. We are still in the holiday season which makes it difficult for some who would like to be here, but who have to replace absentees. Still we have a nice mixture and we look forward to a great week of interchange. I was present at the Niagara Falls Congress. There one became aware of the vast diversity of people who follow the Carmelite *Rule,* single hermits, hermits living in community, friars and nuns of both Orders, congregations of women Carmelites, members of Carmelite secular institutes and laity who are drawn to the Carmelite way of life.

On behalf of the Organising Committee and of Sister Máire and the members of the Sisters' Council, I welcome you all to what promises to be a great week of presentations, of workshops, of sharing with each other and of well organised liturgical celebrations.

The Historical Origins of the Carmelite Rule of 1247

Pat Mullins, O Carm

On 1 October 1247, Pope Innocent IV issued his bull, *Quae honorem conditoris*, commanding Carmelites to accept the "proclaimed, corrected, and mitigated" rule (*regula bullata*) he had drawn up for them. The *Rule* was a modified form of the "formula of life (*vitae formula*)" written for the Latin hermits on Mount Carmel by Patriarch Albert of Jerusalem, probably in 1213. Albert's formula of life says that it was written in accordance with the Latin hermits' "proposal (*propositum*)" i.e. in accordance with the way of life they had chosen.

The historical origins of the Carmelite *Rule* of 1247 can therefore be divided into three phases or stages:[1] 1: the establishment of the first Latin hermits on Mount Carmel during the first two decades (1192-1212) of the Second Latin Kingdom of Jerusalem; 2: the composition of a "formula of life (*vitae formula*)" for the hermits by Patriarch Albert of Jerusalem (c.1213); 3: the modification of Albert's formula of life (*vitae formula*) as a Religious *Rule* for the Carmelites after their move to Europe by Pope Innocent IV in 1247.

Before turning to these developments, however, we outline the history of the first three Crusades, the monastic history of Mount Carmel, and the practice of the consecrated life in the Latin Kingdom of Jerusalem, which provide the background to the establishment of the Latin hermits on Mount Carmel.

The First, Second and Third Crusade

During the eleventh century, the Seljuk Turks, one of several Turkish tribes who had embraced Islam (Sunnite rather than Shi'ite), had taken control of the Caliphate of Baghdad and began to extend their influence into the territories of the Byzantine Empire. In 1085, the Seljuks captured the Byzantine stronghold of Antioch in Syria and gained control of Palestine. By 1092, they had captured Nicaea, close to the Byzantine capital, Istanbul, and in 1095, the Byzantine emperor, Alexius I Comnenus, sent envoys asking for help from the West. Responding to this appeal, and to the threat that the Seljuks posed to pilgrims from the West visiting the Holy Land, the army of the First, so-called "People's Crusade" captured Jerusalem in 1099 and a Western-style feudal kingdom of Jerusalem was established in the following year. The thirteenth-century collection of laws, known as the *Assises de Jerusalém*, provided for such things as the king's officers, the administration of justice, the collection of taxes, the granting of fiefs, provisions for military service, and the regulation of trade. They show that, in addition to the nobles and their families who had settled in the Latin kingdoms during the Crusades, a substantially larger number of persons was classified as bourgeois and had their own "courts of the Bourgeois" under the *Assises de la cour des bourgeois*, which reflect the traditions of Roman law operating in Southern France at that time.

By the middle of the twelfth century, the Crusader strongholds in the Near East had become increasingly vulnerable and, when Edessa was taken in 1144, urgent pleas for aid soon reached Europe. In 1145, Pope Eugenius III issued a formal crusade bull, the first of its kind, launching the Second Crusade. Following an unsuccessful attempt to take Damascus in 1148, an uneasy truce was established. When one of his caravans was attacked in breach of this truce, Saladin, the leader of the Saracens, proclaimed a holy war *(jihad)* against the Latin Kingdom of Jerusalem. At the Battle of the Horns of Hattin, in 1187, his armies defeated the Crusaders and, as a result, the Crusader territories were reduced to a narrow strip along the coast.

By 1190, a Third Crusade had been organised, led by King Philip II Augustus of France and Richard I (the Lion-Heart) of England. In 1191, after capturing Cyprus *en route*, Richard assisted in the siege of Acre, which eventually fell to the Crusaders. In September 1192, Richard and Saladin signed a treaty of peace to last five years that would give pilgrims free access to the holy places. The Third Crusade had failed in its major objective, the capture of Jerusalem, but the possession of Acre and of the coastline from Tyre in the North to Jaffa in the South, permitted the continued existence of a titular kingdom which became known as the Second Kingdom of Jerusalem.

Monasteries on Mount Carmel

The area usually designated as Mount Carmel is a range of hills and valleys running for some 34 kilometers southeast of the present-day port of Haifa, with the river Kishon to the North. It was during the first two decades (1192-1212) of the Second Latin Kingdom of Jerusalem that the first Latin hermits established themselves on Mount Carmel. The caves at the Wadi 'ain es-Siah, about 2 km inland from the point of the promontory on the western side of Mount Carmel, where the Latin hermits settled, had previously been the site of a Byzantine settlement known as the monastery of St Elisha.[2] Archaeologists have shown that it had been used as a monastery at various times from about AD 570 but that it had been abandoned for some time when the Latin hermits came. There were a number of other Greek and Byzantine monastic sites in the area.[3] To the north, there was a Greek monastery dedicated to St Margaret the Virgin (near the site of the present lighthouse).[4] Also to the north, near the cave of Elijah on the lower slopes, was the then recently established Monastery of Elijah, a community of Greek-speaking hermits who settled there about 1155. We know of two other monasteries on Mount Carmel, one Byzantine and one Greek, in the area to the south known as St John of Tyre.[5]

All these various Eastern-rite monastic settlements were based on the Palestinian "laura". According to Friedman, the "laura" was the most characteristic form of monastic life during the 6th and 7th centuries, when Palestine was considered the centre of Christian monasticism. It consisted of a group of cells in which the hermits lived beside each other, rather than in common, and where, rather than living subject to a rule, each hermit was independent and bound only by his moral subjection to his superior. During the week, the hermits lived a solitary life but on Saturdays and Sundays they came together for the liturgy, to collect the raw materials for their basket-making, to arrange the barter or sale of the baskets they had woven, and to discuss issues pertaining to the group as a whole.[6] Mosca notes that, in Palestine, the mountain laura was the more common form[7] and Friedman says that many lauras used large caves as chapels and that many caves, including some in the settlements in the Wadi 'Ain-es-Siah, had cisterns for holding water.[8]

The Latin Hermits on Mount Carmel

A Latin Patriarchate of Jerusalem had been established after the First Crusade in 1099. The Patriarchate had a Latin ecclesiastical organisation and hierarchy under a Latin patriarch, Archbishop Daimbert of Pisa. The forms of consecrated life then typical of Europe at that time quickly established themselves in the Latin Kingdom of Jerusalem and there were a number of Benedictine, Clunaic, and Cistercian monasteries, as well as foundations by the Canons of St Augustine and the Norbertine (Premonstratensian Canons).

By the middle of the twelfth-century, groups of Latin hermits had established themselves at various places in Palestine, including Galilee, Jerusalem, Jericho, the mountains of Mount Tabor, the Black Mountain, and the Quarantena, and at Palmarea near the foot of Mount Carmel.[9] These hermits were under obedience to the abbots of local monasteries and contemporary ecclesiastical legislation forbade them to live the solitary life "without a superior *(sine majore inspectore)*."[10]

None of the available sources prior to the period after the third Crusade (1187-1192)[11] refer to Latin hermits on Mount Carmel[12] and suggestions in some documents that Latin hermits had settled on Mount Carmel before the 1192 treaty between Richard the Lion Heart and Saladin, are now generally regarded as historically inaccurate. An account by the Dominican Etienne of Salagnac (1210-1291), written about 1278 but surviving only in a copy made by the Dominican, Gernardo Guido, in 1305, refers to an intervention by Aimerico Malafaida, the Latin Patriarch of Antioch, in relation to hermits on Mount Carmel. This account is now thought to have confused the hermits on Mount Carmel with those who lived on the Black Mountain and mixed up Aimerico, Latin Patriarch of Antioch, with Albert, Latin Patriarch of Jerusalem.[13] Bagatti has dated the pottery found at the Wadi 'Ain-es-Siah site to the period 1200-1250 approximately[14] and the excavations conducted by Roehricht confirm that a monastery had been built there during the thirteenth century on the site of a slightly earlier, more modest hermitage.[15] Both of the monastic settlements excavated by Roehricht were of the laura kind: there were separate cells for the hermits, the cell of the prior was located at the entrance, and there was an oratory in the middle of the cells. Scholars are agreed that the earliest likely date[16] for the first of the two settlements would seem to be 1192. This was the year in which King Richard I (the Lion Heart) of England signed a treaty with Saladin that drastically reduced the Crusaders' territory but which gave pilgrims access to the Saracen-held holy places in Jerusalem.

The accounts written by pilgrims in Palestine during the thirteenth century indicate that there were two possible routes from Acre where the ships from Europe disembarked, to Jerusalem, their most important destination. One route went inland towards Galilee in the east and then south to Jerusalem, and the other took the coastal route south before turning east to Jerusalem. The location of the first Latin settlement on Mount Carmel was close to this coastal route. The itinerary known as *Les Pélerinages et Pardouns de Acre* describes the first stage of this route (Acre to the cave of Elijah at el-Kadr near the foot of Mount Carmel, crossing the Kishon river and visiting Palmarea, Frenchville, and Haifa *en route)* as being four leagues (i.e. 4 hours of walking, about 12 miles).[17] From the cave of Elijah via the monastery of St Margaret the Virgin, to "the Carmel" (i.e. the settlement of the Latin hermits at the Wadi 'Ain-es-Siah) was another league (an hour's walk, about 3 miles). Noting that the settlement at the Wadi 'Ain-es-Siah was on the main coastal route to Jerusalem from Acre (less than half a league, half an hour's walk, from the road), that it was one of the places on the route where visitors were welcome, and that the other Latin hermits in Palestine often looked after pilgrims, Friedman suggests that the Latin hermits on Mount Carmel may have seen hospitality to the pilgrims going to Jerusalem as an important part of their calling.[18]

The Latin Hermits' "Proposal"

Albert's "formula of life" says that it was intended to be "in keeping with" the hermits' "proposal" (*juxta propositum vestrum tradamus vobis vitae formula),* i.e. in keeping with their proposal to follow Christ as hermits on Mount Carmel. The word "*propositum*" is usually[19] translated as "*proposal*"[20] or "avowed purpose"[21] and, according to Bede Edwards, it refers to "the proposal to follow Christ according to the recognised observances of the eremitical life,"[22] i.e. the decision to follow the stable form of eremitical and ascetical life[23] that the hermits had already adopted and which they were already living at the time they asked their Patriarch to compose a formula of life for them. The reference in the prologue to the *formula of life* to their settlement being near the spring of Elijah *(juxta fontem in monte Carmeli)* may be used to suggest, not only that they would draw their water from a source used also by the prophet Elijah, but also that, spiritually, their proposal was inspired by the solitary lifestyle of that prophet. Such was the conclusion drawn by Jacques de Vitry, bishop of Acre from 1216-1228, when he described the Carmelites as "following the example and living in imitation of the holy and solitary man, Elijah the prophet (*ad exemplum et imitationem sancti viri solitari Eliae prophetae*)"[24] after visiting the site.[25] The *formula of life's* description of their settlement conforms to what archaeologists have discovered at the site: the "hermits *(eremitis*)" had separate cells (*singuli vestrum*

singulas habeant cellulas separatas), the larg
Prior, presumably) was nearest the entranc
oratory in the middle of the cells (*oratoriu*
medio cellularum).

Who were these first Latin hermits to
Carmel? Joachim Smet suggests that Latin he ... else-where in Palestine may have moved to Mount Carmel for safety following the drastic reduction in Crusader territory after the battle of the Horns of Hattin in 1187.[26] The importance of the site associated with Elijah and Elisha near Latin hermitages in the Jericho region may have made Mount Carmel an attractive alternative if this were the case. Friedman suggests that they may have been Latin hermits who had moved there from Calabria.[27] C. Cicconetti uses the term "lay brothers-pilgrims-hermits (*conversi-pelegrini-eremiti*)" to describe them and he sums up their "proposal (*propositum*)" as having made a personal, rather than juridical, option to "live in holy penitence *in obsequio Jesu Christi*" i.e. to live "in holy penitence as pilgrims in the Holy Land ... as his [Jesus Christ's] vassals, subject to his obedience and his law." Living in the land where Jesus Christ had lived, and recognising him as "the Lord of that land (*dominus loci*)," they owe him their obedience and faithful service and, for this reason, proposed to dedicate their lives "to living as his vassals (*in obsequio Jesus Christi*)."[28]

V. Mosca comments that, since they included both clerics and non-clerics, it would be more accurate to describe them as living a lay type of life rather than to describe them as "lay brothers (*conversi*)." He also suggests that, although it was personal for each one, their proposal was common (in the sense of being equal for all of them).[29]

St Albert of Jerusalem (1150-1214)

It was the Italian-born Latin Patriarch of Jerusalem, Albert of Avogadro (1150-1214), later known as Albert of Jerusalem, who wrote the formula of life for the Latin hermits on Mount Carmel. Born in the diocese of Parma, he lost his parents as an adolescent oved to Mortara, then an important centre of education d culture. He became one of the first canons regular of [the Holy Cross of] Mortara, in the province of Pavia, when that Congregation was founded in 1180, and was prior of the local community in Mortara. The communal life of the canons was based on prayer, work, poverty, penance, silence, fraternity and the nourishment of the Word of God.[30]

Albert was made bishop of Bobbio in 1184 and less than a year later, in 1185, he was appointed to Vercelli where he spent twenty years (1185-1205) as bishop. In 1191, he held a diocesan synod whose disciplinary decrees had a significant impact and remained in force until about 1600. In 1194, he wrote the new statutes for the canons of Biella, whom he addressed as "beloved brothers in Christ (*dilectis in Christo fratribus*)," a form of address remarkably similar to that found in the formula of life he wrote later for the Carmelites. As president of a commission of three, Albert was asked by Pope Innocent III to investigate how the *Humiliati*, a charismatic and poorly organised group that had emerged in the South of Italy, might be "integrated under a single regular proposal (*conformaretis in unum propositum regulare*)". Having met with, and heard, the views of the *Humiliati*, he drew up a "formula of life (*vitae vestrae formulam*)"[31] for the first, second, and third orders of the *Humiliati* that was approved by the Pope in 1201.

Appointed as Patriarch of Jerusalem in 1205, the 56-year old archbishop settled at Saint Jean d'Acre early in 1206. During his time as Patriarch, Albert was principally concerned with keeping the peace among the leaders of the Crusades, supporting Jean de Brienne, whom he had crowned as King of Jerusalem-Acre in 1210, negotiating the release of the Patriarch of Antioch when he was kidnapped, and negotiating peace and the exchange of prisoners with the Sultans of Egypt and Damascus. In 1213, the Pope invited Albert to participate in the Council of Lyons in 1215 but, 14 on September 1214, when he was taking part in a procession for the Feast of the Holy Cross, he was stabbed to death by the master of the Hospital of the Holy Spirit whom he had deposed as not worthy of the post.

Albert of Jerusalem's Formula of life for the Hermits (c.1213)

At some point during that, his time as Patriarch (1206-1214) Albert composed the "formula of life (*vitae formula*)" for the hermits on Mount Carmel. Mosca thinks 1213 the most likely date because of the time needed for Albert to get to know the hermits before legislatively approving their *propositum*, and because there is no record that Albert ever got around to informing Pope Innocent IV of this approval despite their frequent communications.[32]

Albert's "formula of life (*vitae formula*)" for the Carmelites is a short document that respects the way of life that the hermits had already been living for the previous 15-20 years while, at the same time, ensuring that they were not isolated from each other or from the life of the church. In the prologue to the *formula of life,* Albert addresses the hermits on Mount Carmel as "his beloved sons in Christ (*dilectis in Christo filiis*)," a form of address similar to that used for the statutes of the Canons of Biella in 1194. He describes himself as having been called by God to be Patriarch of Jerusalem, (*Albertus Dei gratia vocatus Patriarcha*), suggesting that it was because of his paternal jurisdiction over those who belonged to the Patriarchate of Jerusalem that he was writing a formula of life for the Latin hermit-brothers on Mount Carmel.[33] Different approaches have been taken as to the likely intended structure of Albert's formula of life. Traditionally, remaining in the cell unless otherwise occupied was seen as its core but Bruno Secondin has suggested that the cell and the eucharist should be recognised as the two *foci* of the Rule.[34] In 1996, Enzo Mosca posed an interpretation based on seven sections constructed as an arch, with the reference to the eucharist in the middle and the other sections mirroring each other from a practical and spiritual point of view.[35] The following outline is based on Mosca's approach.

A1 (The following of Christ)

The first section (A1) presents the Carmelite way as, first and foremost, a life of allegiance to Jesus Christ (*in obsequio Jesus*

Christi vivere). In the thirteenth century, the word "*obsequium*" was widely used to denote feudal and military service and, in the context of the Crusades, it suggests the acceptance of Jesus Christ as Lord and protector, and living a life of loyal service to him.

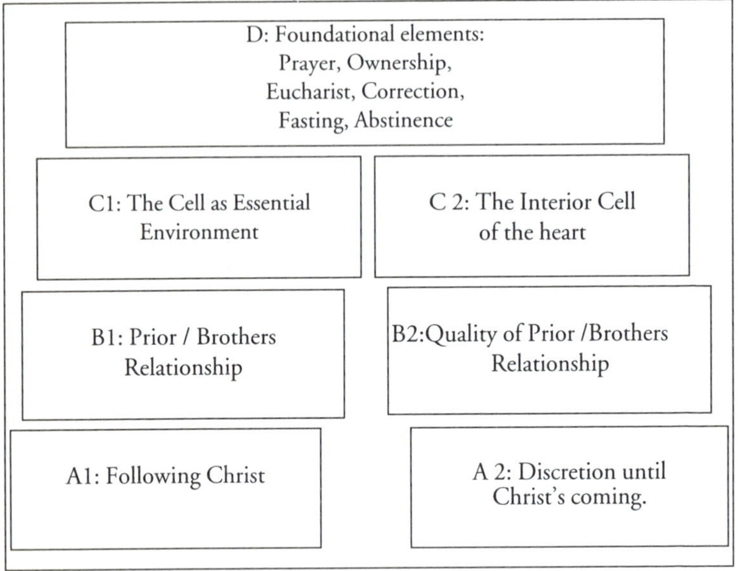

B1 (The relationship between the Prior and the Brothers)

The second section (B1) presents the relationship between the Prior and the Brothers. While the Carmelites are described as "hermits *(eremitis)*" in the first section, they are referred to as "brothers *(fratres)*" in this and in the following sections. They are to live as brothers, under obedience to a prior elected from among them "by unanimous assent (*ex unanimi assensu*)" or by the "greater and maturer part (*maior et sanior pars*)." The prior (chapter 4) is the first among equal brothers whom he is called to serve.

C1 (The Cell as the structure and essential environment of this Way of Life)

The third section (C1) presents the cell as the basic structure and essential environment of this way of life. Each one is to have their own cell (*singoli vestrum singulas habeant cellulas separatas)* allotted by the Prior and each is to "remain in his cell or near it, mediating day and night on the Word of the Lord and keeping vigil in prayer (*die ac nocte in lege Domini mediantes et in orationibus vigilantes*), unless he is occupied with other lawful activities. ... The Prior's cell is to be near the entrance so that he can meet with whoever comes."

D (Foundational Elements:
Prayer, Ownership, Eucharist, Correction, Fasting, Abstinence)
The fourth section recognises the following six elements as foundational elements of this way of life: 1: the recitation of the canonical hours, or a prescribed number of *Our Fathers* instead; 2: renunciation of all personal property and holding everything in common (*nullus fratrum dicat sibi aliquid esse proprium, sed sint vobis communia);* 3: having an oratory in the middle of the cells for daily Eucharist (*mane per singulas dies ad audienda missarum sollemnia);* 4: loving fraternal correction (*caritate media corrigantur)* and discussion of "matters of discipline and spiritual welfare"; 5: daily fasting from September to Easter when this was possible, recognising that "necessity overrides every law (*necessitas non habet legem)";* 6: abstinence from meat.

C2 (The interior Cell of the Heart)
The fifth section (C2) corresponds to the third section (C1) on the cell, and highlights the spiritual values that should dominate in the interior cell of each one's heart: the spiritual battle against evil, work, and silence. The hermits are to clothe themselves in God's armour in order to withstand the trials that put their allegiance to Christ to the test and the underlying, and recurring theme in the description of "God's armour" is that meditation on the Word of God both saves us (see Prov 2:11) and tells us the means by which we can be saved. In response to the problems of boredom and negativity, Albert proposes that the hermits dedicate themselves to work of some kind and cultivate silence and the proper use of the tongue.

B2 (The quality of the Prior-Brothers Relationship)
Just as the fifth section (C2) outlines the spirituality of the interior cell, parallelling the description of the exterior cell in the second-section (C1), so the sixth section (B2) corresponds to the second section (B1) by highlighting the spiritual values that should underlie and characterise the relationship between the Prior and the Brothers. The Prior's role is one of service to the others: "whichever of you would be first must become your bondsman." The Brothers, in turn, are to "hold your Prior in humble reverence (*priorem vestrum humiliter honorate*), your minds not on him but on Christ who has placed him over you."

A2 (Discretion Until the Coming of Christ)
Section seven (A2) parallels the first section (A1) on living in allegiance to Christ by looking forward to the return of the Lord at the end of the world when he "will reward anyone who does more than he is obliged to." As a balance to excess, it recommends that "the bounds of discretion are not exceeded ... for discretion is the moderator of virtue."

The Fourth Latern Council (1215)
The Fourth Lateran Council of 1215 banned the formation of new religious orders unless they accepted the *Rules* of St Benedict, St Augustine, St Francis or St Dominic. Since they followed none of these rules, the Carmelites found themselves in a difficult situation even though they had received their formula of life from Albert, the Patriarch of Jerusalem, before that Council was celebrated. Had Albert of Jerusalem not been murdered in 1214, he would have attended the Council and it seems likely that the Carmelite *Rule* would have been included among the Rules of Religious Life that the Council accepted as normative. Despite the difficulties caused by the exclusion of their particular way of life from the list of approved Rules at Lateran IV, the Carmelites were able to have their way of life approved by Pope Innocent III before he died in 1216. Ten years later, their formula of life was again approved by Innocent's successor, Pope Honorius III,

in his *Ut vivendi formam* which was addressed to "the prior and hermit brothers of Mount Carmel."[36] Three years later, in 1229, Pope Gregory IX, who was an admirer and confident of St Francis of Assisi, imposed an absolute Franciscan form of poverty on the Carmelites. They were prohibited to own land, houses or other revenues, except male asses, and a small amount of livestock or poultry so as to enable them to remain free for the contemplation of the things of heaven and to take up the struggle against the powers of evil, renouncing all the things of earth. Soon afterwards, the Saracens began to get the upper hand against the Crusaders so that fewer and fewer pilgrims came to the Holy Land. Apparently because of economic problems, and because of the threat of the Saracens, the community decided in 1238 to leave Mount Carmel and return to Europe. This meant renouncing their original intention to follow Christ as hermits in the Holy Land and to adapt this intention to different circumstances in Europe. Very soon after they left Mount Carmel, there were foundations in Cyprus, Sicily, England and France. Living in isolated places away from cities and towns, survival became increasingly difficult and they found themselves in great economic difficulties. In 1245, Pope Innocent IV approved Albert's *formula of life* and recognised the difficulties of the Carmelites by granting an indulgence to those who gave alms to them.

Pope Innocent IV's Carmelite Rule (1247)

Following the [first] General Chapter of 1247, held at Aylesford, delegates were sent to Pope Innocent IV with the request that Carmelites be allowed to change their status and pass "to a state to where they could have the joy of being useful to themselves and to others." In effect, they were asking the Pope to allow them to adapt themselves to the norm of mendicants like the Franciscans and Dominicans but, in such a way as to retain their own particular charism. In response to this request of the General Chapter, on 1 October 1247 Pope Innocent IV issued his *Quae honorem Conditoris* approving a modified version of Albert's *formula of life* as a rule of religious life. The Papal bull commanded the Carmelites to accept the "proclaimed, corrected, and mitigated" rule *(regula bullata)* he had drawn up for them.

To bring them into line with the emphasis on the three vows of poverty, chastity and obedience (then a relative novelty to the Franciscans and Dominicans), an explicit mention of chastity and the renunciation of ownership are added where the Brothers are told to promise obedience to their Prior. The concession allowing the brothers to have male asses and a certain amount of livestock or poultry in Pope Gregory IX's *Ex officii nostri* (4 April, 1229) was incorporated into the *Rule* but the prohibition on owning anything, even in common, was changed. Recognising that their form of common ownership was different from the absolute poverty of the Franciscans, the Carmelites were allowed to make and own new foundations, even in cities, "If the Prior and brothers see fit (*secundum quod Priori et fratribus videbitur expedire*)." An addition was made allowing the Carmelites to take their meals in a common refectory while listening to a reading from scripture. All who could were now to join those in holy orders to say the canonical hours, rather than say them on their own. When travelling outside their own houses, food prepared with meat could now be taken "so as to avoid giving trouble to your hosts" or when at sea. The time of the nightly silence was also shortened, beginning now after Compline, rather than after Vespers, and ending after Prime, rather than after Terce of the following day.

Development and Continuity

Noting the different ways in which Joachim Smet, Carlo Cicconetti, and Bruno Secondin interpreted the effect of the changes introduced by Pope Innocent IV in Albert's formula of life,[37] Vincenzo Mosca argues that a strong element of continuity can be discerned as the original charism gradually assumed its definitive form. He describes that element of continuity as a "semi-hermit lifestyle oriented toward the cenobitical (*un semi-eremitismo indirizzato verso il cenobitismo*)" and says that the development was creatively faithful to this charism under the authorative guidance of the Apostolic See.[38] Mosca's recognition of the role played by the Apostolic See in the gradual evolution of the charism echoes the words of Vatican II's *Lumen gentium* 43 where it describes the role of the hierarchy in relation to the evangelical councils:

> While the Holy Spirit is the guide, the authority of the church has itself been at pains to interpret the evangelical counsels, to regulate their practice, and also to set up stable forms of living them.

The guiding role of the Holy Spirit, and the important interventions of both Albert, the Patriarch of Jerusalem, and Pope Innocent IV, in the evolution of the charism from the original proposal of the Latin hermits, through Albert's formula of life to Pope Innocent IV's Carmelite *Rule* of 1247, are now widely recognised. The modified eremitism oriented towards fraternity of its original manifestation in the Latin hermits proposal, the limited cenobitism acknowledging the importance of both the physical and the interior cell in Albert's *formula of life*, and the adaptation of Albert's *formula of life* to the norms of the Friar movement in Pope Innocent's *Rule*, are among the most significant early milestones of the Carmelite way. They both mark the important states on the journey and point forward towards what lies ahead.

The capacity to adapt to very different circumstances in the light of pastoral needs under the guidance of the Spirit is, perhaps, one of the great threads of continuity in our Carmelite charism and it is this aspect that our 1995 Constitutions highlight in the final section of the chapter on "The Gift and Mission of the Order."

> As the human race enters into a new period of its history, we seek, as Carmelites inspired by the Spirit at work in the church, to adapt our way of life to new conditions. We seek to understand the signs of the times and to examine them in the light of the gospel, of our charism and of our spiritual heritage, so that we may incarnate this way of life in different cultures.

Notes

1. See the distinction between the *Propositum*, the *Vitae formula*, and the *Regula bullata*, in Vicenzo Mosca, *Alberto Patriarca di Gerusalemme: Tempo - Vita - Opera* (Rome: Edizioni Carmelitane, 1996) 443.
2. See Mosca (n. 1) 437; E. Friedman, *The Latin Hermits of Mount Carmel. A Study in Carmelite Origins* (Rome, 1979) 74-75.
3. Apart from those listed by name, there were also others: See Mosca (n. 1) 437. See also Friedman (n. 2) 91-95; ibid, "The Medieval Abbey of St Margaret of Mount Carmel," *Ephemerides carmeliticae* 22 (1971) 295-348.
4. See Mosca (n. 1) 437; Friedman (n. 2) 84-91.
5. See Mosca (n. 1) 437; Friedman (n. 2) 80-81.
6. See Friedman (n. 2) 100-101.
7. Mosca (n. 1) 437.
8. See Friedman (n. 2) 101.
9. See J. Bale, *De praeclaris ord. Carm scriptoribus ac theologis catalogus* (London, British Museum, Ms. Harley 3838) ff. 157r-157v; Joachim Smet, "Gerard of Nazareth" in *Dictionnaire d'histoire et de géographie ecclésiastiques* (Paris, 1984) 20:783-784; *The History of Jerusalem ad 1180,* translated by A. Stewart (London, 1896) 26-27.
10. See B. Z. Kedar, "Gerard of Nazareth. A Neglected Twelfth Century Writer in the Latin East," *Dumberton Oaks Papers* 37 (1983) 74; Mosca (n. 1) 398-399.
11. See Joachim Smet, *The Carmelites* (Barrington Ill, 1975) 1:3-8; Friedman (n. 2) 104-105; Mosca (n. 1) 399.
12. See Kedar (n. 10) 65; Mosca (n. 1) 398.
13. See E. Friedman, "Uno squardo ulteriore sulle origini del Carmelo" in AA.VV., *Le origini e la regola del Carmelo* in *Quademi Carmelitani* 2-3 (1987) 3-250 at 86-93; Kedar (n. 10) 70; Mosca (n. 1) 396-399.
14. See B. Bagatti, "Relatio de excavationes archeologicae in Monte Carmelo," *Analecta ordinis carmelitarum discalceatorum* 3 (1958) 277-288; 6 (1961) 66-70; 7 (1962) 127-130. See also Damian of the Cross (Eugenia Nitowski) OCD, *The 1987 Preliminary Season in the Wadi-es-Siah (*Salt Lake City, Carmel of the Immaculate Heart of Mary, 1987); D. Pringle, "Thirteenth-Century Pottery from the Monastery of St Mary of Carmel," *Levant* 16 (1984) 91-111.
15. See Friedman (n. 2) 168-169; Mosca (n. 1) 440.
16. See Smet (n. 11) 1:3-8; Friedman (n. 2) 104-105; Mosca (n. 1) 399.
17. See Friedman (n. 2) 156. See also H. Michelant and G. Raynaud, *Itinéraires à Jérusalem et descriptions de la Terre Sainte, rédigés en francais aux XI, XII et XIII siècles* (Genève, 1882) 229.

18. Friedman (n. 2) 104-105.
19. In the light of St Jerome's *Epistles* 52,5, it might also be translated as "religious profession," see *The Rule of St Albert,* Vinea Carmeli 1 (Aylesford-Kensington, 1973) 79 n. 7.
20. According to M. Maccarrone, the word *propositum* at that time, referred to "the will to dedicate oneself to a state of higher Christian life without specifying whether consecrated by a vow or religious profession." See M. Maccarrone, "Riforma e sviluppo della vita religiosa con Innocenzo III," *Revista di storia della Chiesa in Italia* 16 (1962) 47 n. 44.
21. See *The Rule of Saint Albert,* Vinea Carmeli 1 (Aylesford-Kensington, 1973) 78-79.
22. See *The Rule of Saint Albert,* Vinea Carmeli 1 (Aylesford-Kensington 1973) 78 n. 7.
23. See Carlo Cicconetti, *La Regola del Carmelo: Origine, natura, significato* (Rome, 1973) 99.
24. See Jacques de Vitry, *Histoire Orientalis* 52 in *Gesta dei per Francos,* edited by J. Bongars (Annover, 1611) 1:1074-1075.
25. See Mosca (n. 1) 450.
26. See Smet (n. 11) 1:5; Mosca (n. 1)436.
27. See Friedman (n. 2) 173.
28 . See Cicconetti, (n. 23) 100-101, 106.
29. See Mosca (n. 1) 444.
30. Chapter 23 of the Rule of the Canons of Mortara included the following: *"Praepositorum cura sit ut subditorum mentes Scripturarum, lectionibus assidue muniant, ne lupus invisibilis adytum inveniat quo ovile Domini ingredi et aliquam ovium surripere valeat."* See Mosca (n. 1) 205 n. 164.
31. See Mosca (n. 1) 352
32. See Mosca (n. 1) 445.
33. Cicconetti rejects the view that Albert was acting as papal legate, rather than as Patriarch of Jerusalem, in approving the formula of life of the hermits on Mount Carmel, see Cicconetti (n. 23) 110. Mosca holds that, whether as Patriarch or papal legate, Albert would have been acting as a local bishop from the perspective of a strict interpretation of canon law. A case could be made for the view that Albert was exercising the quasi-papal authority of Patriarchs at that time or that he considered himself the *alter ego* of the Pope as papal legate. Ruling out neither view, Mosca highlights the paternal role of the Patriarch in the formal recognition of charisms, as outlined by Kees Waaijman and Hein Bloommestijn, "The Carmelite *Rule* as a Model of Mystical Transformation" in AA. VV. *The Land of Carmel* (Rome, 1991) 61-90, and by Bruno Secondin, "What is the Heart of the Rule?" in AA. VV., *Albert's Way: The First North American Congress on the Carmelite Rule,* edited by Michael Mulhall (Rome: Carmelite Institute, 1989) 93-132. Mosca suggests that Albert might be best considered as the founder of

the group of hermits on Mount Carmel, see Mosca (n. 1) 452-456.
34. See Secondin (n. 33) 93-132.
35. See Mosca (n. 1) 462-468.
36. See N. Geagea, *Maria Madre e decoro del Carmelo: La pietà mariana dei Carmelitani durante i primi tre secoli della loro storia*. Institutum Teresianum, Studia 4 (Rome: Teresianum, 1988) 96.
37. See Mosca (n. 1) 514-518.
38. See Mosca (n. 1) 518-519.

The Carmelite Rule: A Gospel Approach

James McCaffrey, OCD

I am taking as my starting-point a distinction given by Vatican II for a better understanding of the origin of the gospels and using it as an approach to our Carmelite *Rule* (DV 19).[1] We can distinguish three stages in the formation of the gospels:

1. What Jesus did and taught prior to the ascension. This is the Christ-event – the Jesus of time and space and his message in the historical context of his life and death. This first stage is Christ-centred.
2. The handing on (tradition, oral and written) of the Christ-event – Jesus and his message – in the light of the deeper lived experience of it by the early Christian community, enlightened by the Spirit and prior to the writing of the gospels. This second stage is community-centred.
3. Documents written with the evangelists' personal slant and creative expression of the Christ-event – Jesus and his message. Drawing on what was handed on (tradition, oral and written), the authors "selected, synthesised and drew out the implications" in response to a concrete community-situation.[2] This third stage is written documents-centred, records which are carefully shaped by an original insight.

These three stages are inseparably linked to each other and entirely interdependent.[3] If we do not see the gospels in this way, we run the risk of a fundamentalist approach to the word of God, with everything taken literally; or the developing gospel tradition would become a mere creation of the early Christian community, without roots in the historical Jesus.

Contexts

The Word became flesh in a specific, historical context, conditioned in time and space. It is easy from the pages of the gospels to recreate – at least in broad outline – the world into which Jesus was born, with its Semitic language and culture (Aramaic); its imagery, pastoral (sheep, goats, birds, seeds, flowers) and urban (traders, merchants, money, taxes); its idioms (allegory, parable, metaphor, discourse, narrative); its landscape of undulating hills and mountains (Golan, Hebron, Judea, Negev), dotted with towns, large (Capernaum, Bethsaida) and small (Nazareth, Bethlehem); its meandering river (Jordan), inland sea (Lake Galilee) and fertile plain (Jezreel).[4] The social milieu, too, opens up to the keen and observant gospel reader – its political conflicts (freedom-fighters, zealots against tyrannical Rome); religious movements (Sadducees and Pharisees); festal celebrations (Passover, Tabernacles); and a motley assortment of inhabitants (poor, rich, widows, tax-collectors, blind, lame and beggars).[5]

All these are part of so many layers that may have to be peeled away in order to reach the truth enfleshed in Jesus and first proclaimed in one confined part of the world, a teaching destined to spread to the ends of the earth until the close of time and still needing to be incarnated among so many diverse peoples. We call this process *inculturation*, with Jesus and his message always central to it – a whole dynamic process, long, painful and risky. Not for the faint-hearted, the narrow, the closed mindset. But absolutely essential for any community journeying, like the early Christians, into the unknown and open to the work of the Spirit. It is the exodus mentality.

Like the gospels, the Carmelite *Rule*, too, has its own historical context, conditioned as it is in space and time.[6] We find it embedded in a geographical setting similar to that of the gospels and reflecting the political, social and religious concerns of the late twelfth to early thirteenth century. It is a rule of the Holy Land. It has come down to us enhanced by associations with Elijah and the schools of the prophets on Mount Carmel and enriched by its association with the Wadi 'Ain-es-Siah where the

Order was born.[7] That remote solitary range, with its secluded valley, was ideal for the first hermits. However, driven later from this idyllic setting by the advancing Saracens from 1238 onwards and with the expansion of the Order as a result to Europe and later even further afield, Carmelites would be forced to discover in every place a "spiritual" Carmel – an inner solitude, silence and prayer of the heart – in the midst of busy towns and cities.

Many of the first hermits were themselves crusaders impelled by religious fervour to recapture the Holy City from infidel hands. The *Rule* abounds in martial imagery – breastplate, shield, helmet, sword, arrows, cincture – drawn from Paul's Letter to the Ephesians (6:11-17). This extensive use of a warrior's panoply provided western warlike soldiers with a meaningful vocabulary for the "trials" and "persecutions" of the spiritual combat mentioned in the *Rule* (18).[8] Even the replacement of the Pauline "obedience" to Christ[9] with the phrase "allegiance" *(obsequium)* to him (2) is evocative of the feudal system widespread in the Palestine of the *Rule* – "allegiance" from "ad," meaning "towards," and "liege," meaning "feudal lord" or sovereign of vassal subjects. This same phrase profoundly characterised medieval Christianity at the time of the crusades.[10] In the *Rule*, however, there is no suggestion of slavish surrender redolent of blind or unquestioning obedience, even to Christ. The document allows for both dialogue and community discussion (15) which are attuned to a more nuanced understanding of obedience. Both of these are envisaged in the *Rule*.

Another example of historical context: the *Rule* is a male document, written by a man for men. It would be more than two hundred years before women were admitted to the Order (1452). Some more sensitive accommodation to the concerns of women today may be required.[11] An Order of the Brothers of Our Lady of Mount Carmel could possibly reflect more explicitly in some way the presence of Sisters, too, by the use of inclusive language.

The *Rule* also emerges out of the maelstrom of political conflicts of the day between the warring Saracen and Christian faiths. The assassination in 1214 of Albert, the Latin patriarch and author of the *Rule*, and his residence in Acre rather than in Jerusalem which was then under Muslim control, bear telling witness to those turbulent times in which the *Rule* was written.

Christocentric

The *Rule* of Carmel, like the gospels, is christocentric. It is the pervasive use of scripture that seems for the most part to make it so.[12] "The new is hidden in the old," Augustine wrote, "and the old is made manifest in the new," while Jerome wrote, "Ignorance of the scriptures is ignorance of Christ."[13] Conversely, to know and love the scriptures is to know and love Christ. Albert is one who speaks and thinks explicitly in biblical terms, and the document itself is a mosaic of biblical texts; it reflects the style of a discourse from Matthew even more than that of a legal document. Scripture quotations abound, explicit and implicit, at first sight apparently disproportionate in our *Rule* which is the most diminutive among its peers.

In its extensive use of biblical quotations, the *Rule* is following the tradition of St Basil, exemplified in his *Moralia*, the collection of scriptural sentences that forms the basis of his own *Rule*. He did not include one word of his own, believing that any human addition would be superfluous to the word of God. Still more radically than Basil, the desert fathers refused to have a rule altogether, fearing that it would foster servile observance characteristic of the Old Law and thus preclude the freedom of the gospel; hence their decision to preserve their charism not by laws but by living examples.[14] Likewise, the first Carmelites began by being themselves a living rule – indeed, a living word.

"The word of God," we are told, "must abound in your mouths and hearts" (19). And anticipating the words of Vatican II – that "prayer should accompany the reading of sacred scripture" (DV 25) – the *Rule* continues, "Let all you do have the Lord's word for accompaniment" (19). Littered with scripture texts, the document disposes the Carmelite, mind and heart, to be saturated with Christ's presence through his word. The focus of our prayer is "pondering the Lord's law" (10) – that is, the word; a "listening together … to a reading from holy scripture" is prescribed for mealtimes (7); the assurance that "holy meditation will save you" is also there (19, Prov 2:11); a reminder that "the sword of the Spirit [is] the word of God" (19) comes with an explicit reference to what "Our Lord says in the gospel" (21) and to the inspired teaching of Paul "into whose mouth,"we are told, "Christ put his own words" (20, see 2 Cor 13:3). This apostle, in turn, is quoted explicitly at length with a glowing endorsement of work through his own example, "toiling night and day," and with a warning against "restless idlers" (20, 2 Thess 3:7-12).

But perhaps even more significant than all this, the person of Christ embraces the whole document. Apart from several explicit references to Christ throughout, the initial greeting, "health in the Lord," is followed immediately by an implicit reference to Hebrews with the words, "many and varied … ways" (2, Heb 1:1), evoking God's final and definitive revelation in his Son. This, in turn, is followed by a description of religious life, indeed of the vocation common to all the baptised, as essentially a following of Christ.[15] The *Rule* gradually unfolds, and the typical Carmelite prayer of "pondering the Lord's law day and night" (10) is directed implicitly to the person of Christ who replaces the law (Jn 1:17); the next phrase, "keeping watch at his prayers", also opens up implicitly a further perspective on the return of Christ. The movement then comes back full circle again from Christ at the beginning to Christ at the end, with a large inclusion bracketing and uniting the whole document: the *Rule* concludes explicitly evoking the parousia, "Our Lord, at his second coming" (24). In addition, the prescription, unknown to the ancient desert monks, for a daily celebration of Mass binds the religious into one, a living community gathered around the eucharistic Lord (14).

Hence, the importance of the first preliminary stage in the formation of the gospels for a better understanding of the Carmelite *Rule* as essentially christocentric. And the need to strip it, where necessary, of archaic dress, outdated structure(s) and the spatial limitations of a historically-conditioned document, if the core message of Carmel is to extend like the gospels and take root through inculturation in a vast variety of places and times.

Community

But there is much to be learnt, too, from the second stage in the formation of the gospels for a better understanding of the *Rule*: the focus on community. The church is a living community in Acts growing, under the action of the Spirit, in its understanding of Jesus. There we see the essential traits of an ideal early Christian community. Vatican II has restored a fresh vision of church by shifting the emphasis from a pyramid, triangle or hierarchical structure back to its self-understanding as *communio*.[16] The evangelists give expression to this early community lifestyle, already existing before the gospels themselves were written. So, too, with the *Rule* of Carmel. It gives a legal framework at the request of the first Carmelites to their specific way of life which was already a lived community experience, or charism, before ever it was codified in writing – "a rule of life [*formula vitae*]," we are told, "in keeping with your avowed purpose [*propositum*]"or plan (3). The lawgiver of Carmel is clearly inspired by the Jerusalem model of the church in the early chapters of Acts: the sharing, friendship, joy, freedom, openness, dialogue, listening to the word, a multi-faceted church of varied charisms and ministries, pulsating with the breath of the Spirit impelling it to growth and expansion.

Even a cursory glance at Acts confirms these observations. There the community is united "mind and heart" in the bond of mutual love (Acts 4:32). This primacy of love is everywhere affirmed. The believers were united in this way because "they devoted themselves to the apostles' teaching and fellowship, to the breaking of bread and the prayers"(2:42). These virtues emerge as basic and perennial Christian values. They are reaffirmed of the community a second time in Acts: "Attending the temple together and breaking bread in their homes ... praising God" (2:46-47).

But the ideal of the early Christian community is no starry-eyed vision. Some of the early hermits came to the Holy Land as penitent pilgrims. Others were warring crusaders. For these, the recapture of an earthly Jerusalem was to give way to the conquest of a heavenly one. The way forward was still beset with obstacles and called for vigilance, perseverance and defensive weapons. Albert first quotes Job: "man's life on earth is a time of trial" (18, Job 7:1). This requires spiritual weapons, for the devil is always "on the prowl like a roaring lion", the *Rule* reminds us, echoing Peter (18, 1 Pet 5:8). So the writings of Paul on the spiritual combat are taken up again in the *Rule* with striking relevance: "clothe yourselves in God's armour" (18, Eph 6:11). The Carmelite community, like the early Christian community, is a fragile one in need of God's weaponry which Albert insists must, in Paul's word, be put on.[17] Our defences, then, are God's gift; he clothes the community with his own strength.

"Faith" is the "shield" for all occasions without which "there can be no pleasing God", we are told; and hope of salvation is the "helmet" providing the basis for trust (19). This armour of God is in turn at the service of *communio*, directing the Carmelite, the *Rule* says, "to love the Lord your God with all your heart and soul and strength and your neighbour as yourself" (19, Dt 6:5; Mt 19:9; 22:37-39). In this relentless battle, then, the theological virtues of faith, hope and love are God's armour – his powers – and take pride of place. Carmelite asceticism is primarily God's work, not ours. But it is also closely linked with human endeavour. Albert insists on "work"; it comprises more than one third of the *Rule*. He further links it with silence, which again enhances *communio*: "Sin will not be wanting where there is much talk" (21, Prov 10:19). The Carmelite is to "watch and pray" – a phrase in the *Rule* evoking the Gethsemane scene: "Watch and pray that you may not enter into temptation" (Mt 14:38). "Watch and pray" – alert, vigilant and always ready to brandish the weapons of God in defence of the common life. Admonished in this way both by scripture and the *Rule*, the Carmelite is called to put on the armour of God like a sentinel on guard, to remain constant in faith, to keep kindled the flame of love in community and to rely in hope on the promise of a heavenly Jerusalem.

Two further points of contact between the cenobitical Carmelite lifestyle and the early church community might be worth mentioning. We recall that in the Jerusalem community "no one claimed private ownership of any possessions, as everything they owned was held in common" (Acts 4:32). From communion of hearts within that community flowed a common sharing of goods, without social distinction or divisive self-interest. Such is the spiritual demand of radical poverty required of those united "mind and heart". The *Rule* of Carmel, too, enjoins renunciation of possessions as an exercise of *communio* in almost identical terms: "None of the brothers must lay claim to anything as his own, but you are to possess everything in common" (12, Acts 4:32; see 2:44). The radical poverty of the *Rule* is an expression of fraternal sharing in love.

Albert, like the author of Acts, gives prominence to the eucharist – for him, a focal-point in the community; to prayerful listening with the scriptures – making Christ present; and to prayer – with its still-point in the person of Jesus who embodies "a new law," replacing the literal "law" of the Lord in the *Rule*: an inner law written on human hearts by the Spirit of the living God (2 Cor 3:2-3). We might add, with reference to the Our Father recommended in the *Rule* (11), that it is a "compendium of the whole gospel" and of "heavenly doctrine".[18] To pray is to praise and petition God with the mind and heart of an ecclesial community-prayer such as it was for Teresa. It is reassuring to find all three elements – scripture, eucharist and prayer – in Albert's vision for his new community. These are values that give a distinctive stamp to our Carmelite life.

Such a lifestyle embodied in the *Rule* highlights the importance of the second preliminary stage in the formation of the gospels for a better understanding of Carmelite life as essentially community-centred – modelled on the shared communion of the early church, and already a lived experience before it was ever a written document.

Written Word

Likewise, there is much to be learnt from the third stage in the formation of the gospels for a better understanding of the *Rule*: the focus on a written document shaped by an original insight. The gospels have their own special literary form. So, too, has the *Rule*. It follows the contemporary literary-form of a Letter[19] – a standard framework giving ample scope for considerable flexibility of content and variation of people addressed. It is directed not just to Brocard,[20] but also to "whoever may succeed you as Prior" (22) and is a legal document. Albert was well-versed in juridical matters; he was also thoroughly informed about the then current movements of religious life. And so, the Patriarch of Jerusalem was admirably equipped to write the *Rule*.

The gospels are an intricate web of diverse strands of tradition, oral and written, fused delicately into what appears, at first sight, a seamless robe. So, too, Albert's *Rule* is interwoven with traditions that already preceded and shaped it, although these are never expressly mentioned in the text. The reference to "the spring of Elijah" (1) evokes a long oral tradition centred on the fiery prophet of Mount Carmel, who is now in a real sense father and founder for all Carmelites, wishing to live in his spirit.

The text is also influenced by the *Rule* of Augustine (the *Rule* followed by the Canons Regular of the Holy Cross of whom Albert was one) and by the *Rule* of Benedict, with its monastic tradition. "Our saintly forefathers" mentioned in the Carmelite *Rule* (2.11) would embrace such classical spiritual authors as Cassian (his *Conferences*), Basil and Jerome. Albert and the Carmelites, however, did not adopt any of the already existing *Rules*. They opted for a new contemporary concept – a way of life between the monastic orders and the laity in general. So, the *Rule* bears its own original stamp and is a creative expression of a new form of religious life.

This new lifestyle already existed, with its own inner life of growth, development, expansion and adaptation before the *Rule* gave it legal form. The definitive document emerged from an intensely lived experience of Carmelites striving to discover their own identity during the first forty years of their history. We can trace the successive stages of their search in the *Rule*. First, they were hermits living solitary lives in the Wadi 'Ain-es-Siah under their leader, Brocard, occupying separate cells, reflecting on scripture and devoting themselves to prayer. They later became hermits living in community under a prior, with structures to preserve their common sharing of the eucharist, food and other goods. Finally, through forced expansion to Europe and through changed circumstances, they opted for the lifestyle of mendicant friars, with ministries such as preaching and the public celebration of the eucharist. These three religious strands have spawned family tensions and conflicts down the ages, but they are inseparably linked at the deepest level of what it means to be a true Carmelite. Albert achieved a balanced and harmonious blend of all three. In this lies the originality of his *Rule*.

1. Eremitical lifestyle

The stress on the eremitical aspect emerges clearly – prayer, keeping vigil, silence, solitude, separate cells, pondering the scriptures.[21] Their ultimate purpose is inner transformation. The Carmelite is called to be a hermit at heart. Such is the deeper dimension of the *Rule*. At the outset, Albert directs the Carmelite to Jesus Christ and faithful service of him "pure in heart" (2). The word, heart, already opens up an inner space where the exercises and safeguards of the solitary life take on depth and purpose. Listening to the scriptures allows "The sword of the Spirit, the word of God" to penetrate the deep heart's core (19). The solitary allows the word to question experience, and experience in turn to question the word. Carmelites are called to know the scriptures from the inside: "the word of God must abound in your mouths and hearts" (19, Eph 6:17; Col 3:16; Rom 10:8).

Consider the originality of Albert's stress on silence. Within the tradition of religious life, there is no other rule which reserves, comparatively speaking, so much space for silence. It is indicative of Albert's insight. The legislator who is so succinct elsewhere is expansive here. The four basic exercises surrounding the cell are described in two lines: remaining, watching, praying, meditating (10). But silence has two hundred and ninety-nine words devoted to it, while faith, hope and love have only seventy-two. Moreover, Albert is astute in his choice of scripture texts throughout the *Rule* – selecting, synthesising and drawing out their implications (to borrow the terms of Vatican II about the task of the evangelists).[22] Nowhere, perhaps, is he more discreet and discerning than in the cluster of scripture texts he chooses in support of silence (21, e.g. Is 32:17; Sir 20:8; Mt 12:36). All are in view of his personal stress on intimacy and quiet communion alone with God.

But the heart of the eremitical life is not silence in itself; silence is the atmosphere that must envelop it. Neither is it the cell. We are not just dealing with a material dwelling-place; the cell is the visible symbol of an inner shrine with space for God. The *Rule* rightly exhorts: "your breast [must be] fortified by holy meditations" (19). At the centre of the empty room is the risen Christ and a Spirit-filled pray-er focused on the word in quiet expectation of the second coming: "pondering the Lord's law day and night and keeping watch" (10). The eremitical aspect of the *Rule* bears the stamp of Albert's original touch.

2. *Cenobitical lifestyle*

Since Vatican II, a renewed understanding of community in terms of interpersonal relationships has been paramount.[23] This, as we shall now see, is reflected in the *Rule*. It also helps us to discern some specific characteristics of Carmelite community which highlight the shift from a dominantly eremitical lifestyle to a newly-emerging cenobitical one.

The life in common is to be leavened by prayer, scripture reading, solitude and silence – all typical of the eremitical life. But there is also work to be done in common, for the most part in silence, while preserving the bond of love. This new family of friends will work from within the word of God: "Let all you do have the Lord's word for accompaniment", says the *Rule* (19, see Col 3:17; 1 Cor 10:31).

The emphasis on the community leader as "prior" (4.9.12. 22.23) has considerable significance. He is not an abbot, for example who is chosen for life. He is a brother among brothers. His role is described in gospel terms as a loving service of others – a superior, we are told, who makes Christ present in the community: "Whoever pays you heed pays heed to me" (23, Lk 10:16).

In the midst of the cells there is to be a common oratory bringing the community together for the daily celebration of Mass (14). All the separate cells are thus united, through mutual bonds of love, into a temple of living stones built around a eucharistic presence at the centre of the community. A common refectory, too, is prescribed where the religious are to gather for a shared meal and prayerful listening to the scriptures (17).[24] Besides this, the "indiscretions and failings of the brothers ... should be lovingly corrected" in a common gathering (15).

There is a specific community dimension to the panoply of spiritual defences in the Letter to the Ephesians, from which Albert borrows copiously. The reference to the "cincture" in God's armour is recalled in the *Rule* using the apostle's own words: "Your loins are to be girt" (19, Eph 6:14). The "girded loins" evoke the expectant watchfulness of a soldier on guard. This ties in admirably with the end-time perspective in Albert's stress on "watching in prayer" (10). But the image also comes to us rich with connotations of the exodus-meal to be eaten "with a girdle round your waist" (Ex 12:11). It evokes the vision of a praying Carmelite community in exile on a collective pilgrimage, faced with obstacles and difficulties but determined to share in the victory of the new passover.[25] The imagery would have had special significance for many of the first hermits who came as pilgrims to the Holy Land, eventually to settle on Mount Carmel; there they continued the penitential life on which they had already embarked while in Europe, as part of the movement known as "The Poor of Christ".[26] This imagery would, in turn, take on additional significance when the first community was later exiled from the Holy Land.

It is worth noting, however, that the *Rule* has no reference to the soldier's "footwear", also mentioned in the spiritual armour of Ephesians (6:15). A mention of this could too easily be seen to open a perspective as yet foreign to Carmelite life at this earlier stage of its development. Albert's *Rule* might be misconstrued because of it in terms of Isaiah's words: "How beautiful upon the mountains are the feet of the messenger who brings good news and announces peace!" (52:7). This would be a premature interpretation, implying that behind the first hermits-in-community there were evangelists, with feet shod in readiness to proclaim the gospel worldwide in the spirit of the mendicant orders. Only later did Innocent IV, with his definitive approval of the *Rule* in 1247, give the mendicant spirit its official place in the Carmelite charism. To this aspect of the *Rule* we now turn our attention.

3. Mendicant lifestyle

A comparison of the original text (1206-14) with the later one, "corrected, emended, and confirmed" by Innocent IV (1247), highlights subsequent redactions of Albert's *Rule* – omissions, additions, modifications, relaxations and improvements – in the light of changing circumstances. The earlier version was a flexible text open to growth, movement and the new life-experiences of the community. We should read the definitive *Rule* too with the same spirit, open in our approach to the charism it enshrines, ever searching for a deeper understanding of it and always ready to adapt to new needs and changing conditions. Even Albert's apparently stringent version, "You are always to abstain from meat, except as a remedy for sickness or excessive feebleness", is later modified by Innocent IV who dropped both the "always" and the "excessive" (17). So, too, fasting is prescribed, though with the clause "unless [for] bodily sickness or feebleness, or some other good reason" (16). To this we may add the permission granted later in the definitive *Rule*: "At sea, however, meat may be eaten" (17) – a mitigation which pointedly describes the changed situation of Carmelites with new foundations abroad and the necessity of travel by sea. These modifications and mitigations are an application of the *Rule*'s more general principle for the distribution of common goods to each religious according to "whatever befits his age and needs" (12); likewise, "need is not bound by law" (16).

We have a highly significant exception to Albert's instruction on remaining in the cell, which he tempered by: "unless attending to some other duty" (10). This "duty", literally "lawful activities", is not specified. But it must surely qualify as work, explicitly referred to a few paragraphs later: "You must give yourself to work of some kind, so that the devil may always find you busy" (20). Again, the work is unspecified. But the emphasis on work is endorsed by Innocent's addition and conclusion to the whole section: "That is the way of holiness and goodness: see that you follow it" (20). We have here an important stress on being occupied, in contrast to being idle. So, we find already in embryo the later extension of "lawful activities" to the ministry of mendicant friars. Hardly a seismic shift, however, or a quantum leap – even the reactionary and uncompromising Nicholas the Frenchman, of *The Flaming Arrow*, had to concede that the hermits on Mount Carmel went out to preach from time to time![27]

Forced to return to Europe, the Carmelites resonated with the mendicant movement. The *Rule*'s accent shifted to embrace the demands of a new ministry in view of a different culture. Innocent's reduction of the night-silence from "after Vespers until Terce" to "after Compline until after Prime" (21) was most likely an accommodation to the pressing demands of this new lifestyle. The point of gravity in the new society had shifted from the countryside to the cities. This was part of the "signs of the times" and called for adaptation.[28] It did not matter whether a monastery was located on Mount Carmel or across the seas, in a solitary place or in a city, provided it was essentially a true

Carmel, regardless of the circumstances. But it could only be such, if the *Rule*'s essential elements were preserved untarnished – the eremitical, community and apostolic dimensions – with whatever priority or emphasis the religious chose to give them. They all flowed from the hidden spring of the word, pondered and assimilated in praying hearts, and were all three inseparably linked in the Carmelite charism.

Pondering with Mary[29]

So far, we have made no reference to Mary. Her silence in the gospels is reflected in the silence of the *Rule*. She is the Spirit-filled woman of prayer silently "pondering" the word which she "treasured" in her heart (Lk 2:19.51). Her prayer is the heartbeat of every praying Carmelite, "pondering the Lord's law day and night" (10). The term "pondering" comes to us from the first psalm. It is deeply laden with the rich implications of the bible's wisdom and apocalyptic traditions, associated with obscure mysteries awaiting further clarification. It connotes puzzling over something that still needs understanding.[30] Mary kept the enigmatic words of the angel in her heart, awaiting their final unfolding through the light of the Spirit in God's time. But the prayer of "pondering" involves not only grasping the meaning of obscure sayings. It also requires us to live by them, putting them into practice. It calls for openness to God and to the strangeness of his ways. Mary is attentive to God's time for the full revelation of the mystery entrusted to her, pondering it continually without ever fully grasping it. As the first disciple of her Son,[31] she is called to constant surrender to God's word – wonder, surprise, bewilderment, anxiety, concern, pain. Clothed in Mary's scapular, Carmelites put on her mind, heart and prayer. We ponder the richness of our *Rule* with her, always searching for its relevance here and now, open to new ways of living it and understanding its hidden, mysterious meanings in the light of the Spirit.

Moving with the Spirit[32]

The greeting at the beginning of the *Rule*, "blessings of the Holy Spirit" (1), would seem to be designed precisely for that purpose: to dispose recipients for openness to the Spirit. And we read, in the final paragraph of the *Rule*: "Our Lord, at his second coming, will reward anyone who does more than he is obliged to do" (24). Then Albert withdraws from the scene. He has captured the charism in legal terms, as far as it is possible. For the rest, a vast silence, like the silence of the gospels, descends and opens up space for the Spirit. The written word is not a "sacred and untouchable" text exhausting all the possibilities of Carmelite living, nor is it a dead letter.[33] So much of the charism can never be adequately expressed in rules and regulations. But quickened by the Spirit, the *Rule* becomes a many-faceted text, always open to deeper understanding like the gospels, and admitting new forms of Carmelite life in response to the "signs of the times".

Looking at the *Rule* in this light, we are reminded of the gospel teaching: "[The Spirit] will bring back to your memory everything that I have spoken to you" (Jn 14:26). This recalling is not just to remind Carmelites of the letter of the law. The Spirit will point out the relevance of the text here and now as time unfolds. The concluding silence of the *Rule* bears the same message as the gospels: "I have yet many things to say to you but you cannot bear them now" (Jn 16:12). The words of the *Rule* await the further light of the Spirit. "He will make known to you the things that are to come" (Jn 16:13), we are told in the gospels. The perspective widens into an unknown future of growth, expansion and development. It is the same Spirit who will lead us into all truth (Jn 16:13) – the full richness of our charism that can never be adequately expressed in words. That charism is embodied in a definitive *Rule* but our grasp of it is always partial.

Besides, the Spirit works in a "spiral" movement,[34] advancing new possibilities for anyone who, as the *Rule* says, "does more than he is obliged to do" (24), inviting us constantly to reassess our calling in changing times, but taking us back again and again to the criterion of the *Rule*: the admonishment, with its final words, to use "common sense [which] is the guide of the virtues" (24). There is great originality and freedom in the way the *Rule* is slanted by Albert and later by Innocent IV. But for a balanced interpretation of everything "over and above", we must return repeatedly to the essential elements – the eremitical, the community and the apostolic aspects.

Good works, good works, is the acid test for Teresa,[35] action in the gospel sense of whoever "hears the word of God and does it" (Lk 8:21). Witness the recent highly-successful event of the Joint Carmelite Forum meetings with participation by all branches of the family accepting and respecting the difference of emphasis that distinguishes one group from another.[36] Each lifestyle is the fruit of a profound and prayerful listening to the *Rule* in the light of the Spirit. "Look to the future, where the Spirit is sending you", wrote John Paul II in *Vita consecrata*, "in order to do even greater things" (110). This is the "more", the "over and above" of which the *Rule* speaks. The church is filled with the wonders of the Spirit, who "breathes where he wills" (Jn 3:8). The family of Carmel must be ready at all times to expect the unexpected from God.

Notes

1. DV = *Dei Verbum* (Dogmatic Constitution on Divine Revelation).
2. "The sacred authors wrote the four gospels, *selecting* some things from the many which had been handed on by word of mouth or in writing, reducing some of them to a *synthesis, explicating* some things in view of the situation of their churches ..." (DV 19; italics mine).
3. For a scholarly exposition of this approach to the gospels, containing the English text of the *Instruction Concerning the Historical Truth of the Gospels* (1964), see Augustin Cardinal Bea, *The Study of the Synoptic Gospels: New Approaches and Outlooks* (English version edited by Joseph A. Fitzmyer, London and Dublin: Geoffrey Chapman, 1965); also Raymond E. Brown, *Reading the Gospels with the Church: From Christmas through Easter* (Cincinnati, Ohio: St Anthony Messenger Press, 1996), pp. 9-20 and 87-90.
4. As an aid to entering and recreating Palestine in the time of Jesus, see Jerome Murphy-O'Connor, *The Holy Land: An Oxford Archeological*

Guide from Earliest Times to 1700 (Oxford and New York: Oxford University Press, 1998).

5. To understand the culture and milieu into which Jesus was born, see Seán Freyne, *The World of the New Testament* [New Testament Message 2] (Wilmington, Delaware: Michael Glazier, 1980).

6. I wish to acknowledge my debt to such pioneering studies as: Michael Mulhall (ed.), *Albert's Way: The First North American Congress on the Carmelite Rule* (Rome: Institutum Carmelitanum/Barrington, Illinois: The Province of the Most Pure Heart of Mary, 1989); *The Rule of Carmel: New Horizons* (Rome: Editrice "Il Calamo", 2000); and the masterly study, Kees Waaijman, *The Mystical Space of Carmel: A Commentary on the Carmelite Rule* (Leuven: Peeters [The Fiery Arrow Collection], 1999).

7. For the origins of the Order, see Wilfrid McGreal, *At the Fountain of Elijah: The Carmelite Tradition* (London: Darton, Longman and Todd, 1999); Elizabeth Ruth Obbard, *Land of Carmel: The Origins and Spirituality of the Carmelite Order* (Leominster: Gracewing, 1999).

8. References to the *Rule* follow the numbering of points as agreed by the O Carm and OCD General Councils; see letter of Joseph Chalmers, O Carm and Camilo Maccise, OCD, January 30th, 1999.

9. " Obedience of faith" is an expression characteristic of Paul (Rom 1:5; 16:26), defining faith as obedience. This concept is taken up again by Vatican II: see DV 5.

10. Carlo Cicconetti, *La Regola del Carmelo: Origine – natura - significato* (Rome: Institutum Carmelitanum, 1973), p. 44.

11. For a woman's perspective on the *Rule,* see Anne Henderson, "Rereading the Rule Today: A Woman's Viewpoint," in *The Rule of Carmel: New Horizons,* op. cit., pp. 143-53.

12. On the biblical implications of the *Rule,* see Camilo Maccise, "Biblical Spirituality in the Rule of Carmel", *Carmelite Digest* 17/1 (2002), pp. 12-32; Giovanni Helewa, "The Word of God and the Rule of Carmel," in *The Rule of Carmel: New Horizons,* op. cit., pp. 21-44; *The Word of God and the Rule of Carmel* [Ongoing Formation 5] (Rome: Casa Generalizia Carmelitani Scalzi, 1996).

13. See *Quaest. In Hept.*, 2,73 and *Commentary on Isaiah*, Prol. respectively.

14. Points well made by Dom O. Rousseau, "The Call to Perfection in Patristic Tradition", in *Vocation* [Religious Life II] (London: Blackfriars, 1952), pp. 8-9.

15. The following of Christ is the "fundamental norm" and "supreme law" of the whole Christian life and so of the consecrated life. See *Perfectae caritatis* (Decree on the Appropriate Renewal of the Religious Life) 2.

16. The church is a mystery and as such, this *communio* is presented in a variety of metaphors. See *Lumen Gentium* (Dogmatic Constitution on the Church) 6-10.
17. 18-19. As a Pauline metaphor for putting on Christ and being transformed in him through baptism, see Gal 3:27; Rom 13:14; Col 3:10; Eph 4:24; 2 Cor 4:16.
18. See Tertullian, *De oratione* 1 and Cyprian, *De dominica oratione* 9 respectively. For an excellent study of the Our Father, with special emphasis on the end-time perspective which fits admirably into the whole thrust of the Carmelite *Rule*, see Raymond E. Brown, "The Pater Noster as an Eschatological Prayer," *Theological Studies*, 22 (1961), pp. 175-208.
19. See Waaijman, op. cit., pp. 5-6.
20. The original register of Innocent IV in the Vatican Archive (21, f.465 v) and the oldest manuscripts simply carry the initial 'B'. It was later interpreted as "Brocard".
21. This theme of pondering the sciptures in Carmel has been developed in a variety of recent articles. See note 12.
22. See note 2.
23. See *Lumen gentium* (Dogmatic Constitution on the Church) 6-17.
24. For a modern continuation of the practice of *lectio divina* in community, see the articles of Brigeen Wilson: "A Living Power Among Us: A New Springtime of the Gospel", *Mount Carmel*, 49/2 (2001), pp. 8-17; "A Living Power Among Us: Called Together by the Word," *Mount Carmel*, 50/1 (2002), pp. 27-35.
25. For the implications of Carmelite life as a collective pilgrimage, see the seminal articles of Emmanuel Nnadozie: "The Carmelite Rule in Dialogue with the African Continent", in *The Rule of Carmel: New Horizons*, op. cit., pp. 59-76 (especially p. 71); "The Carmelite Rule in Dialogue with Africa: History, Tradition(s) and Gospel Values", *Mount Carmel*, 50/1 (2002), pp. 15-22; "The Carmelite Rule in Dialogue with Africa: A Way of Transformation", *Mount Carmel*, 50/2 (2002), pp. 34-41.
26. In the eleventh century, Western Europe experienced a renewal of eremitical life and an extensive religious movement with the aim of following Christ in his poverty. Its adherents called themselves "The Poor of Christ". People resolutely renounced the world (*conversio*) in order to dedicate themselves totally to God in a life of penitence (*vivere in sancta poenitentia*). Pilgrimages to the Holy Land were regarded as the highpoint of the penitential life. The hermits of Mount Carmel were part of this movement. See Waaijman, op. cit., pp. 2, 7.
27. The importance of *The Flaming Arrow* is outlined in John Welch, *The Carmelite Way: An Ancient Path for Today's Pilgrim* (Leominster:

Gracewing, 1996), pp. 27-38.

28. On the need for creative fidelity and adaptation in the light of the "signs of the times", see Camilo Maccise, "The Future of Carmel – A Reflection", *Mount Carmel*, 49/1 (2001), pp. 19-26.

29. Note recent works on the Marian tradition of Carmel: Donald W. Buggert, Louis P. Rogge and Michael J. Wastag (eds.), *Mother, Behold Your Son: Essays in Honor of Eamon R. Carroll, O Carm* (Washington, DC: The Carmelite Institute, 2001); John F. Welch (ed.), *Carmel and Mary: Theology and History of a Devotion* (Washington, DC: The Carmelite Institute, 2002); Joseph Chalmers, *Mary the Contemplative* (Rome: Edizioni Carmelitane, 2001); Emanuele Boaga, *The Lady of the Place: Mary in the History and in the Life of Carmel* (Rome: Edizioni Carmelitane, 2001).

30. The implications of these wisdom and apocalyptic traditions are developed in Raymond E. Brown, *The Birth of the Messiah: A Commentary on the Infancy Narratives in Matthew and Luke* (Garden City, New York: Image Books, 1979), pp. 429-31. See also Francis J. Moloney, *Mary, Woman and Mother* (Homebush, NSW: St Paul Publications, 1988), pp. 23-7.

31. Mary is the first disciple of her Son. See Encyclical Letter of John Paul II, *Redemptoris Mater* (Mother of the Redeemer) n. 20; Apostolic Exhortation of Paul VI, *Marialis cultus* n. 35.37; Raymond E. Brown, "Mary in the New Testament and in Catholic Life", *America*, May 15th, 1982, pp. 374-9.

32. For a comprehensive treatment of the Paraclete passages in John's gospel, see Ignace de la Potterie and Stanislaus Lyonnet, *The Christian Lives by the Spirit* (New York: Alba House, 1971), Chapter III, "The Paraclete," by de la Potterie, pp. 55-77.

33. See Camilo Maccise and Joseph Chalmers, "Open to God's Future, Circular Letter of the Superiors General, OCD and O Carm, on the occasion of the 750th anniversary of the definitive approval of the Rule of Carmel by Innocent IV" (Rome, 1997), p. 5.

34. This "spiral" movement is typical of the general style of the fourth evangelist, of which the Paraclete passages provide an excellent example. See Ignace de la Potterie and Stanislaus Lyonnet, op. cit.

35. See *The Interior Castle* VII 4:6, in *The Collected Works of St Teresa of Avila*, vol. 2 (Washington, DC: ICS Publications, 1980), p. 446.

36. See the Joint Carmelite Forum issue of *Mount Carmel*, 49/3 (2001).

St Teresa and the Rule of Carmel

Eugene Mc Caffrey, OCD

Among the words spoken by St Teresa on her deathbed two are especially memorable, both of them beautiful expressions of her warm personality and vibrant spirituality: "The hour has come, my Spouse," she said, "for you and I to meet",and a little later she joyfully proclaimed, "Thank God, I die a daughter of the church."

But there is another phrase also spoken by the saint just before she died, one recorded by nearly all witnesses. As she was waiting to receive viaticum she turned to those around her and with warmth and maternal love said to them, "For the love of God, sisters, take care to observe the *Rule* and Constitutions." These were not just the words of a dying nun, not even of a dying saint; they were an expression of Teresa's constant advice and admonition to all her communities. Gracián testifies how often he heard her say in the various houses: "read the *Rule* every day and never let it slip from your heart."[1] These words of Teresa still echo down the centuries and are a constant reminder and an invitation to all of us to refresh our spirits continually in the spring of Carmel so that, in her own words, we can "begin always anew".

The *Rule* has a privileged place in the story of Carmel, both as a spiritual document and as a normative/juridical one. It is an inspirational text, "an institutional expression of a commitment to an ideal".[2] It is about a spirituality that is experienced and a way of life that is lived. Carmelite spirituality as such is impossible to define. Not only is the precise date of the *Rule* unclear but there is no one historical person or persons that can be named as founder of the Order. *The Rule* itself is basic and concise.

It has a beauty and simplicity about it that gives it a quality of poetry more than of legislation, a humble, almost domestic expression of a family spirit and charism – "more inwardly in regard to the spirit than outwardly in regard to expression" is how John of St Samson characterises it.[3] The *Rule* of Carmel is the shortest of the great classical rules approved by the church – shorter than that of Augustine, Benedict, or Francis – yet today, eight centuries later, it is still a way of life and a vehicle of religious experience for thousands of women and men all over the world. "It fascinates me," writes Sr Anne of Ware, "that such a large tree should have so simple a root."[4]

My aim is to try to see in what way the *Rule* of Carmel influenced the writings of Teresa of Avila and found concrete expression in the spirituality of the Teresian convents shaped and moulded by her. I will cover three aspects of the subject:

1. St Teresa and the *Rule*
2. The *Rule* in the writings of St Teresa
3. St Teresa and the spirituality of the *Rule*

1. Teresa and the Rule

We know very little about Teresa's knowledge of the *Rule* before 1560. She obviously made her profession according to the *Rule* of Carmel in 1537. In fact, the *Rule* may have been the only internal law in the convent of the Incarnation, as we have very little information regarding any Constitutions existing in the Incarnation at that time.[5] Teresa's desire for prayer and her first beginnings along the road of spiritual conversion were not inspired by her reading of the *Rule* as such but originated in other sources, such as the writings of Augustine, Osuna and Jerome and the influence of her confessors, especially the Dominicans and the Jesuits – and, most of all, by the special favours and graces which the Lord began to bestow on her from 1554 onwards. Thus, what she intuited first, according to Maximiliano Herráiz, was "the spirit of things, the life itself, rather than the desire to live the *Rule*".[6]

Yet the fruit of the first mystical graces she received touched directly on her relationship to the *Rule* and to her Carmelite vocation. Her immediate response found practical expression in her resolution to follow her religious vocation and to keep the *Rule* with all possible perfection *(Life 32,9).*

It was only in 1562, when she started her work on the foundation of St Joseph's that Teresa began seriously to study the *Rule* and consider its implications. Her discovery was gradual and tentative. In the spring of 1562 when she applied for permission to found St Joseph's, she was not even aware that there were other texts, other historical expressions of the same *Rule.* In fact it was Mary of Jesus, foundress of *De la Imagen* convent in Alcalá, who first informed her of the situation. Mary of Jesus was a *beata,* a sister who lives under a rule but does not belong to a community. She could neither read nor write, but she knew the ancient Carmelite *Rule* by heart. She had already founded a convent of Reformed Carmelites in Alcalá. Teresa admits she was ashamed and surprised that an illiterate nun knew more about the *Rule* than she did! From her, Teresa learned for the first time that it enjoined absolute poverty without communal possessions or endowments. "Until then", she writes, "it never occurred to me to found a convent without revenue, since I thought we ought not to worry about bare necessities" (*Life* 35:2). She at once recognised that the *beata* was right.

Teresa had in fact already sent her application to Rome when she made this discovery. For many months she had been struggling against all sorts of opposition to her proposal that the new foundation be established without income. Her basic inspiration was that St Joseph's would be small, characterised by poverty and simplicity. Already she was engaged in a running battle with the municipal authorities in Avila and with theologians and lawyers urging her to change her mind. Only Peter of Alcántara and the constant reassurance of Christ's words helped her to hold out. The discovery of the "primitive *Rule*" was the catalyst that gave her the freedom and assurance to go ahead. From then on, nothing could make her change her mind or shake her resolve. I love her words to the Dominican, Fr Pedro Ibánez – who in all other matters was her great friend and supporter – when he tried to dissuade her with "two pages of refutations and theology": "I have no use for theology," she said to him, "if it does not help me to follow my vocation and the counsels of Christ." (*Life* 35:4)

Immediately on her return to Avila, Teresa sent another application to Rome, requesting a separate Brief that would counteract the deficiencies of the former in relation to poverty, and asking instead that the new convent be established according to the primitive *Rule* of Carmel. This request was granted in a rescript received in December 1562.[7]

So what did Teresa discover, why did it make such a difference to her work as foundress, and what did she mean by the term, "primitive *Rule*"?

There are three stages in the historical development of the Carmelite *Rule*:

***Rule* of St. Albert,** written between 1206 and 1214 for a small group of hermits on Mount Carmel, and approved by Honorius III in 1226, initiated a way of life; it was followed for a period of no more than fifty years.

***Rule* of Innocent IV**, Albert's *Rule* "revised, corrected and mitigated"(*Quae honorem Conditoris, 1247)* at the request of the General Chapter in Aylesford that same year.

***Rule* of Eugene IV,** giving further additions and dispensations, and approved in 1432.

Only the first *Rule* can strictly be called the "primitive" *Rule.* Teresa does not seem at that time to have even been aware of its existence or of the historical background to any adaptations made to it. What she chose was the *Rule* of Innocent IV – the second form, approved in 1247 with its various alterations and additions. She knew no other. This was, she thought, the first *Rule* of Carmel, the primitive *Rule* without mitigation. In this, Teresa was no different from the rest of her contemporaries, most of whom used the same terminology in speaking of the *Rule* of Innocent IV.

Her reasons for choosing it were very definite and deliberate. It gave expression to the Carmelite life as she herself envisioned it.

Teresa had a clear vision of what she wanted for her new convent: "a healthy community life of moderate asceticism, with an emphasis on prayer".[8] After her experience of the fragmentation and dissipation of the Incarnation, two elements were crucial for her: solitude and viable community. She felt the "primitive *Rule*" best expressed these two ideals. Silence and solitude within community were perfectly nuanced in the *Rule* of Innocent and, at the same time, helped to make a definite break with the religious life that Teresa had experienced at the Incarnation. She needed to give a clearly defined style of life to her new community, a life shaped by her own experience of God and her desire to provide a better balance within community. It also helped her to take a definite stance on poverty, which became a key issue for her in asserting the independence of St Joseph's. Furthermore, it gave authority to her efforts to initiate a much simpler and more creative form of religious life.

The *Rule* of Innocent guaranteed continuity with the past and at the same time allowed for the introduction of something new, fresh and creative. It would be a serious distortion of the work of St Teresa, however, if we consider what she achieved apart from the whole tradition of Carmel as embodied in the *Rule*. Teresa did not give life to Carmel. It existed for four centuries before her and has continued to flourish for another four centuries in a different branch of the Order, independent of her direct influence and charism. "People say this is a new Order", she wrote to Fr Pablo Hernández, "and accuse us of inventing new things. Let them read the first *Rule* of the Order which we observe without relaxation."[9] Even after the juridical separation had taken place, Teresa did not feel the need in any way to remove herself from the historical tradition in which she had been formed.

She did, of course, often use the phrase "the beginning of the Order", referring to the original hermits on Mount Carmel, and at same time to the new beginning in St Joseph's. Thus when Fr Rubeo, Superior General, visited Avila in 1567, he was able to confirm for himself that "the primitive *Rule* was being kept in all its rigour" and "saw a portrait, even though an imperfect one, of the Order at its beginning" (*Foundations* 2:3). He was in no doubt that what Teresa was trying to achieve was not, in any way, a distortion of the original inspiration of the hermits on Mount Carmel, but a return to it. But Teresa was looking for something different, something which, she intuited, already existed in the Carmelite tradition but had been clouded or obscured with the accretion of the years. She wanted to restore the eremitical dimensions so obvious in the original thrust of the primitive *Rule* and at the same time introduce a community dimension that was smaller, more supportive of religious observance than that lived in the Incarnation. In the sixteenth century, no less than today, there were buzzwords. Not dialogue, collaboration, or option for the poor but words equally evocative of the spirit of the age – poverty, simplicity, small communities and personal prayer. These were the ideals for which she was striving. The genius of Teresa was that she was able to create an organic whole out of the various elements embedded in the *Rule* and in the spiritual tradition of Carmel and mould them into a way of life that was both evangelical and contemporary.

This feeling of belonging to the family of Carmel cannot be over-emphasised. There was never a question of rupture but of renewal. The first beginning of Teresa's Reform sprang from the same historical moment and the same spiritual spring that existed at its birth in the thirteenth century on Mount Carmel. The return to the "primitive" Carmelite *Rule* was a clear and explicit choice for Teresa, an essential condition of living her vocation, as she understood it, in the sixteenth century. She felt that she had recovered something that had been lost, and simply wished to live that life and share that experience with others.

2. The Rule in the Writings of St Teresa

There are over sixty references to the *Rule* in the writings of St Teresa (over sixty more than in those of St John of the Cross, who does not mention the *Rule* even once!). Her usual expressions are the primitive *Rule*, first *Rule*, *Rule* of the Virgin, and *Rule* of Our Lady of Mount Carmel. It is important to stress again that Teresa came to a deeper understanding of the *Rule*, not through study or reading, but through her own mystical experience. It was her experience of God that drove her to explore more fully the deeper riches of the *Rule*. She struggled to come to terms with what God was asking of her and sought to discover ways in which to express her new understanding of Carmelite life in a juridical and ecclesiastical setting. All references to the *Rule*, therefore, in her writings are a *posteriori* to her desire to live her religious life more generously than she had for the twenty-seven years of her life in the Incarnation. These references are not always explicit, but they are significant and are a solid basis for exploring the connection between the spirituality of Teresa and that of the primitive *Rule*.

The *Book of the Life*, written in 1565, records Teresa's personal vocation and the beginnings of her work as foundress. The first explicit reference is found in chapter 36 in her description of the founding of St Joseph's: "We observe the *Rule* of Our Lady of Mount Carmel and keep it without mitigation" (36:26). "With this phrase", Maximiliano Herráiz writes, "Teresa presents her Reform in the Church. It is her identity card".[10] One word in the *Rule* resonated especially with Teresa, the word *poverty*. The *Rule*, as she saw it, gave her the objective security she needed that the convent of St Joseph's should be founded without income and galvanised her resolve against all opposition. Thus she intuited the spirit of the *Rule* rather than its legal prescription, a spirit that resonated with her own mystical experiences to share the poverty of Christ and live in the uncluttered simplicity of the gospel.

With regard to the *Constitutions*, there is no doubt that for Teresa the *Rule* was the more important. The *Constitutions* are an expansion of the *Rule* and an expression of it. They are complementary and dependent on each other, reinforcing the same spirit and ethos. Recurring phrases in the *Constitutions* state, for example, "the *Rule* ordains, the *Rule* prescribes, the *Rule* directs us to observe". And in the *Constitutions* themselves, Teresa states quite simply, "everything must be done in conformity with the *Rule*" (31).

The *Way of Perfection* is generally regarded as her commentary on the *Rule*, written in 1566 for "those who follow the primitive *Rule*". Essentially it is a formation manual, a practical handbook of ongoing formation for her sisters. Twice in the opening pages she makes this clear: "This book contains advice and counsel ... for those monasteries that follow the primitive *Rule* of Our Lady of Mount Carmel." And further on she says: "I would consider as well spent the trouble to which I have gone to ensure that the *Rule* of Our Lady and Empress shall be kept in its original perfection" (3:5).

The core of the *Way of Perfection* is its practical teaching on prayer: "unceasing prayer", Teresa says, "is the most important aspect of our *Rule*" (4:2). She directs her nuns to respond to anyone who challenges their way of life: "Tell him you have a *Rule* which commands you, as it does, to pray without ceasing, and that this is a *Rule* you must keep" (21:10). Once again, the authority of the *Rule* is invoked when it comes to various aspects of community life, especially working in common: "it is important not to be together except at designated times, as is the custom we now follow, and is, in fact, laid down in the *Rule*" (4:9). The nuns are thus excused from having a common workroom, since the precepts of the *Rule* encourages silence, solitude and prayer and "these are the very foundations on which this house is built" (see 4: 9).

Finally, in the *Book of Foundations* and in her *Letters*, we see how Teresa saw the *Rule* as the unifying element for all her convents. It is the bond of spiritual and juridical unity between both nuns and friars, an identifying axis around which she builds her Reform. In the end, it did not matter whether a house was founded with income or without, in towns or in cities, under the jurisdiction of the bishop or that of the Order; what mattered most to her was "that they all live the same way of life as at St Joseph's and all follow the same *Rule* and Constitutions" (*Foundations* 3:18).

From such a brief survey of the saint's writings, we see that they do not offer an 'official commentary' or glossary on the

Rule. But her writings still have validity and shed a clear and authentic light on her own experience of the Carmelite *Rule*. For her it was a progressive movement towards more personal awareness and understanding, from the first discovery of its deeper meaning as recorded in the *Book of Life*, to the practical implications spelt out in the *Way*. Finally, in the *Foundations* and *Letters* we see how the *Rule* was embodied and interpreted in the historical development of the Reform under the direction and guidance of the Mother Foundress herself.

3. St Teresa and the Spirituality of the Rule

In the *Foundations*, Teresa writes: "it is important for the sisters to understand both the meaning of perfection and the spirit of the *Rule*" (see 18:8). It is not words or texts in themselves that give life; it is the spirit that animates the *Rule* that is important. Carmelite spirituality is bigger than any document, even one as seminal as the *Rule*. Carmel is above all, spirit and life. The spirit unites every historical expression of the *Rule* with that small group of hermits who first lived on Mount Carmel. It is the source and the bond linking each phase of Carmelite life whether in the thirteenth, sixteenth or twenty-first century.

Each one will have his/her own idea of what constitutes the core of the Carmelite *Rule*. For most, however, the kernel of the text revolves around three central ideas:

1. Allegiance to Jesus Christ, to follow him "pure in heart and steadfast in conscience" (*Rule* 2);
2. The spirit of contemplative prayer: the injunction to pray unceasingly, listening to the word of God in silence and solitude.
3. Community life within a context of work and silence.

Allegiance to Jesus Christ and the following of him is the central focus of the *Rule*; watchfulness in prayer and community life are the means to express and to foster this reality.

"In obsequio Jesu Christi", allegiance to Jesus Christ – or dedication, commitment, dependence, as it is also translated – is pivotal to the way of life to which a Carmelite is called. Even though the

role of Christ is lightly and gently stressed, without elaboration or explanation, yet it is clearly emphasised and is central to the whole focus of the *Rule*. It is a given. Other spiritualities are much more forthright in their presentation of the role of Christ in their particular way of life. For a Carmelite this is more a presence and awareness, a looking at Christ and even more especially a *living with him:* "unswerving in [his] service" as the *Rule* itself states (2). Christ is the milieu of the Carmelite approach to God, the gospel path of true discipleship. Prayer is the unfolding of this personal relationship of each individual to Christ. One gets the impression that Albert knew that those who asked for a rule of life were already striving to live "pure in heart and steadfast in conscience" and he was more interested in highlighting what must be the central focus of their lives: to follow Christ Jesus and dedicate their whole lives to him.

Turning to Teresa, it is not hard to see the parallel between this emphasis in the *Rule* and the centrality of Christ in her own spirituality. It was in and through the mystery of Christ that she came to a deeper experience of the reality of God. Her life is a remarkable witness to the "unsearchable riches of Christ". The mystery of Christ was not just an object of special devotion and meditation; for Teresa, Christ was everything. The "good Jesus" was the only guide, her sole companion and the source of all truth. He was for her a "living book". For the beginner struggling to enter the door of the first mansion, or the mystic centred in the seventh, "he is the beginning, the middle and the end of all prayer" (see *Life* 13:12); there simply is no other way. In speaking of Christ, Teresa uses every word and image she can think of to express the reality of her relationship with him and the nature of his presence in her life – he is, at one and the same time, brother, friend, guide, spouse, companion, teacher, master and the captain of her soul. It is her way of saying that, in her experience, he is All: the one through whom all blessings come, the true friend, the path and the gate to God (see *Life* 22:6-7).

The second essential strand of Carmelite spirituality is contained in the cryptic phrase, "Each of you is to stay in his own cell or nearby, pondering the Lord's law day and night and keeping watch at his prayers" (*Rule* 10). When we try to unravel this core element of the *Rule* we find a number of characteristics, each intertwined and dovetailing.

A contemplative spirit and a deep sense of God's presence are the basis of Carmelite spirituality. Before a rule can be interiorised and appropriated, there must be some level of personal awareness of the reality of God. The Carmelite *Rule*, indeed any rule of life for that matter, is much more than a set of laws and admonitions; it is a sacred place of the spirit, a "mystical space", as Kees Waaijman calls it, an attitude and a response to a particular call. The *Rule* of Carmel expresses itself in the motto of the Order as "a zeal and a longing for the living God in whose presence I stand". Again John of St Samson captures it clearly when he writes, on the origins of the Order: "religious life [at Carmel] was ... animated by spirit, or rather it was all spirit".[11]

For this reason, prayer in the Carmelite tradition can never simply mean prayer as an *activity* or an *exercise* but as a response to God's presence; something nourished in silence, solitude and purity of heart. The *Rule* faithfully captures this orientation in the simple phrase, "pondering the Lord's law day and night". Two of the oldest and most central images of Carmel are found in the opening paragraph of the *Rule*: the *spring* and the *mountain*. These images will be developed and expanded by Carmelites themselves throughout the subsequent history of the Order: Carmel a place of exploration, for those seeking to "drink of the living water of life" and a path of ascent towards the mountain of God, the mountain of perfection. Both images are still further symbolised in the image of the *desert*. Between the spirit of Carmel and the spirit of the desert there is a living relationship: Carmelite prayer is the desert where the Spirit dwells. This search for God in an absence of imposed forms of prayer, free from methods and techniques, is characteristic of Carmelite prayer from its beginning. Although, from the outside, this may seem vague and obscure, it is nevertheless astonishingly active and dynamic. Here centuries vanish and we return to the perennial source, symbolised and historically rooted in the mountain of Carmel and spring of Elijah.

The fact that Teresa was first and foremost a contemplative cannot be denied. Prayer is, perhaps, the aspect of the spiritual journey most associated with her. In a sense, all her books are about prayer in one form or another. She is, in the eyes of the church, the Doctor of Prayer and it is the fundamental charism she has bequeathed to the church and to the Order.

Prayer, for Teresa, is the whole process of the unfolding mystery of God's life coming to fruition in the human person. In her famous description of prayer she portrays it as "a heart-to-heart conversation with One we know loves us"(see *Life* 8:5). The basic elements are: friendship, love, sharing and the personal relationship. Thus, prayer is essentially contemplative – contemplative in the sense of being one to one, open to God and to the full consequences of his love in our lives; it is a time of listening, of openness and of awareness. For all her efforts to describe the path of prayer and guide her sisters along the "royal road", she knows only too well that it is not contained within a method or a technique. Her focus is no different from that of the *Rule* itself; asking not less than everything, a radical and total option for God. Whereas Albert expresses it as a "pondering the Lord's law day and night", Teresa sees it as an intimate, friendly sharing, something that is personal, frequent and solitary.

The essential qualities necessary for a life of prayer as outlined in the *Way* – the practice of virtue, love, detachment and humility – are expressed with similar insistence in the prescription of the *Rule* about spiritual combat and the armour of God necessary for a life of contemplative prayer. The text on spiritual combat comprises over a third of the *Rule* and is the Legislator's way of emphasising the values essential for a life of prayer: constancy, vigilance and perseverance. These are the very qualities stressed by Teresa: *determined determination,* courage and firm resolution. In the spirituality of the *Rule* and in that of Teresa we are called not only to contemplate Christ but to work for him and do battle with him against the forces of evil. Teresa is at home with the imagery of warfare so familiar to those first hermit monks on Mount Carmel, many of them soldiers trained in the military discipline of the Crusades. A true daughter of Avila of the Knights, she spoke with ease of kings and castles, fortresses and captains of arms. She knew only too well the truth of the statement in the *Rule*, that "man's life on earth is a time of trial"(18), and wanted her nuns to be strong in battle and to acquit themselves like good and faithful soldiers. She knew from experience that if you want to achieve great things for God, it is necessary "to clothe yourselves in God's armour so that you may be ready to withstand the enemy's ambush" (*Rule* 18). In the same way, her wish to foster the spirit of prayer in each house by an atmosphere of silence and solitude is echoed in the directive given in the *Rule*, to "employ every care in keeping silent, which is the way to foster holiness "(21).

Finally, we look at the third essential strand in the Carmelite *Rule*. As we have seen, Teresa chose the thirteenth-century "primitive *Rule*" – the *Rule* of Albert revised by Innocent IV – because it best fitted in with her own vision of Carmelite life. It provided an atmosphere more congenial to silence, solitude and the fostering of a spirit of prayer and, at the same time, allowed for a smaller and more closely-knit community life. In the *Rule* of Innocent, both the eremitical and the cenobitical elements of the religious life are safeguarded. Pondering of the word of God in an atmosphere of silence and solitude are sensitively balanced within a loose structure of community life: the provision of an oratory, daily eucharist, weekly chapter, common refectory, and some form of manual work, for example. Coming as she did from the overcrowded situation at the Incarnation, her two major concerns were to provide an atmosphere of prayer that blended easily with a community life that was small enough to be both caring and supportive. Basically, she wanted to establish a spirit of prayerful silence within a healthy community life, a life that was well balanced, with liturgy in common, shared recreation, but work done alone and in silence.

When Teresa says, "the style of life we follow is that of the hermits" (*Way* 11:4) and asks her sisters "to keep before their minds the true founders, those holy prophets from whom we are descended" (*Foundations* 29:33), she is affirming the *eremitical* inspiration of the *Rule.* When, on the other hand, she speaks of her community as a "college of Christ", "a house of the Virgin" and as a place where "all must be friends with each other, love each other, be fond of each other and help each other" (*Way* 4:7), she is stressing the *cenobitical* aspect of the religious life, life lived in common, inspired by the *"koinonia"* of the first church in Jerusalem. Thus work and silence, both key prescriptions in the *Rule,* are equally enshrined in Teresa's directives for her community.

The relationship between prayer and community, so clearly balanced in the *Rule,* are equally refined in Teresa's understanding of religious life. Contemplative life is not something vague or abstract. It needs to find expression in life lived within the human context. She saw the need for an intimate bond between prayer and life, between the highest mysticism and the gift of self, one that shows itself in love and service. "We should occupy ourselves in prayer not for our own enjoyment but so that we have the strength to serve" (*Interior Castle* VII 4:12). I haven't much time, she told Gracián, for the kind of prayer that does not make us grow in holiness.

By way of conclusion, we can say that Teresa's encounter with the *Rule* of Carmel was gradual and ongoing, something she discovered on the way to a new and more personal living of her religious vocation. For her it was not simply a legal document but an inspirational text, one that was at the same time practical, ascetical and mystical. Teresa was a woman with a mission, and the primitive *Rule* of Carmel gave both objective security and validation to her vision. It had a simplicity and strength that resonated with her own dynamic spirituality. In it she discerned a spirituality, rooted in a tradition stretching back to the school of the prophets, to the towering figure of Elijah and the humble Virgin of Nazareth. Through her creative genius she was able to make an organic whole out of her own unique spiritual journey, set, as it was, within the historical tradition of the Order and embedded in the original soil of Mount Carmel. Through the sheer dynamism of her own personal experience of God and of the things of God, she reclaimed a tradition and remoulded a charism.

Notes

1. See *The Teresian Constitution*, Ongoing Formation 4 (Rome: Casa Generalizia Carmelitani Scalzi, 1996), p. 5.
2. *The Word of God and the Rule of Carmel*, Ongoing Formation 5 (Rome: Casa Generalizia Carmelitani Scalzi,1996), pp. 6 -7.
3. See Paul-Marie of the Cross, *Carmelite Spirituality in the Teresian Tradition*, (Washington, DC: ICS Publications, 1997), p. 24.
4. Anne Henderson, "So Simple a Root: Some Strands of Spirituality in the Carmelite Rule", *Mount Carmel*, 50/1 (2002), p. 8.
5. See *Saint Teresa and the Carmelite Rule*, Ongoing Formation 1 (Rome: Casa Generalizia Carmelitani Scalzi, 1994), p. 7.
6. Maximiliano Herráiz, "The Rule Interpreted by St Teresa and St John of the Cross", in *The Rule of Carmel: New Horizons*, (Rome: Editrice 'il Calamo,' 2000), p. 45.
7. *Saint Teresa and the Carmelite Rule*, op. cit., p. 23.
8. John Welch, *The Carmelite Way, An Ancient Path for Today's Pilgrim*, (Leominster: Gracewing, 1996), p. 63.
9. Letter of 4 October 1578.
10. Herráiz, op. cit., p. 51.
11. See Paul-Marie of the Cross, op. cit., p. 18.

Eastern Dimensions of the Carmelite Rule

Christopher O'Donnell, O Carm

The Carmelite *Rule* has had many interpretations in the course of its history. In the medieval period there was a variety of symbolic readings, one of which, John Baconthorpe's, will be the topic of another lecture in this seminar. The *Rule* became central at the time of the Teresian and later Touraine reforms. Over the centuries a conviction grew that the core of the *Rule* was its article 10 about remaining in the cells unless otherwise occupied.[1] More recently there has been an attempt to see not one central point (R 10=7/8) but two *foci*: the cell and the daily eucharist (R 14=10/12).[2]

Though the *Rule* was given to hermits on Mount Carmel it is generally considered to be a Latin type formulary, though with some roots in the patristic writers such as Cassian and perhaps Basil[3] its possible Eastern dimension is a fraught topic. Earlier writers sought to see the *Rule* as an abbreviation of the *Institutes of the First Monks* ascribed to John the 44th bishop of Jerusalem. It is now generally accepted that the *Institutes* are the work of a 14th century Catalan Carmelite, Philip Ribot. This work of his can be seen more as a development of the *First Rubric* than as arising from the Albertine *Rule*.[4]

There are those who seem quite negative towards any significant Eastern influence on the development of the Order or on the *Rule*.[5] Its author was an Italian Canon Regular of the Holy Cross founded about 1080 at Mortara. He was later bishop of Bobbio and Vercelli, before being appointed as Latin Patriarch of Jerusalem.[6] Against this prevailing orthodoxy there are a few voices that would see affinities between the Albertine *Rule* and the Eastern monastic tradition. One such is the Discalced bishop,

Mgr Jean Sleiman, who himself hails from the Middle East. He sees echoes of, and consonance with, the Eastern monastic tradition.[7] There are also important articles from Sr Elaine [Poirot] a sister in a Greek monastery that shows many parallels between the *Rule* and Eastern traditions, especially monastic.[8] She later presented reflections on the *Rule* by a sister belonging to a Greek monastery.[9] This is also a major study, as yet unpublished, on the whole Eastern dimension of the *Rule* by Elias O'Brien.

I would like to begin our these initial considerations by citing a concluding paragraph of Sr Eliane:

> We have brought up some resemblances among others between the Carmelite *Rule* and Eastern monasticism. Here is the witness of a Greek higoumene or female monk: "I have read with close attention the *Rule* of St Albert and I think it is written in the spirit of the Eastern fathers. Some articles are found exactly in the *Rules* of St Pachomius and in the ascetical *Rules* of St Basil. She then recalled the ancient rules of the 4th and 5th century, ascribed to Saint Anthony, used in Eastern Monasteries. Likewise a theological writer, an archimandrite, when asked about this topic, found the *Rule* of Carmel very consonant with the Eastern tradition.[10]

Mgr Slieman and Sr Eliane have impressively covered some of the parallels between Eastern monasticism and our *Rule*. They have looked particularly at its christological centre, its sense of tradition, the role of the prior and the call to continuous prayer. I shall not repeat their work. I am going to present some key ideas in the spirituality of the Christian East and indicate that these too can highlight aspects of the *Rule* whose significance sometimes may not be fully grasped.

We can approach the issue by some generalisation about the different spiritualities of East and West. Both depend on the New Testament; both treasure it all. But whereas the Latin West will concentrate more on St Matthew's gospel, especially the Sermon on the Mount, the East will focus on the gospel of John. Again, the theology of grace in the West is best reflected in Galatians and the first seven chapters of Romans from which we derive a doctrine of actual grace and faith, whereas the East looks to the text of 2 Peter 1:4 which teaches our sharing in the divine nature and develops a doctrine of divinisation. Likewise, an Eastern approach to our *Rule* will find different affinities to the more usual Latin reading.

Eastern spirituality

Christian spirituality was developed and synthesised mostly in monastic circles during the first millennium. In the West we had Augustine (d. 430) and Gregory (d. 604) both of whom were formed by religious life as well as Benedict (d. ca. 547) the father of western monasticism. The spirituality of the East draws on Origen, an Egyptian ascetic and one of the first great theologians of the church (d. ca. 254), Anthony (d. 356) and Pachomius (d. 346) the fathers of Eastern monasticism, and later from the Cappodocian Fathers Basil, (d. 379), his brother Gregory of Nyssa (d. 395), Gregory of Nazianzus (d. ca. 390), who were all originally monks. A bridge between East and West was John Cassian (d. after 430). He was born in present-day Romania and travelled to monastic sites in the Holy Land and Egypt before founding some monasteries near Marseilles about 415. In his two books of conferences and monastic instructions he sought to present the wisdom of Egyptian monasticism to these communities in Gaul.

In the West we are used to the language, originally Eastern, of beginners, proficients and perfect (Evagrius Ponticus d. 399), or the purgative, illuminative and unitive ways (Plato taken up by 6th century Pseudo-Dionysius). But there are other Eastern ways of considering spiritual growth, which are broader and have some greater clarity. The main lines of the spiritual journey were outlined by Evagrius and the Pseudo-Macarius (d. ca. 390). Cassian sat at the feet of Evagrius and later brought his doctrine to the West.

The spiritual journey is above all described as spiritual warfare, which has three key elements.[11] The enemies who incite this warfare have already been unmasked in scripture: the world, the flesh and Satan (see Romans and 1 John). The spiritual journey is firstly a struggle against demons. As one writer puts it: "Just as shadows follow bodies, so temptations follow the commandments."[12] The ascetics were called "strugglers" (*agônistai*). The demons are overcome by discernment, that is identifying their presence or operation, and by custody of the heart. The second element of the combat is custody of the heart. The heart is the battleground in the spiritual struggle; evil is always in danger of penetrating our heart. To avoid being led astray we need discernment and careful examination of conscience. Discernment was both a spiritual art and the fruit of experience. We find an echo of Eastern discernment in the phrase about "weighing our words in a balance" (*Rule* 21 = 16/18). Again, we could easily pass over the three references to the heart in the *Rule*, but they are very significant. We are to follow Jesus with a pure heart (R 2 = Prol./2); we are to love God with our whole heart (see Mt 22:37) and the word of God is to be abundant in our hearts and mouth (R 19 = 14/16).

The third element of this warfare is the struggle against the eight evil thoughts: gluttony, fornication, love of money, melancholy or frustration (*lupé*), anger, listlessness (*akêdia*), vainglory and pride. These were taken over by Cassian and were adapted to produce the Western well-known seven deadly sins. The way to deal with these thoughts was by the scripture, having an appropriate word to attack each one. The monks collected an armoury of such texts; Evagrius collected 487 of them in his *Antirrhhêtikos* (against, counter-speaking). Remember the sword of the Spirit, which is the word of God, the only offensive article in the *Rule's* spiritual armour (R 19 = 14/16)?

In the spiritual path there are three characteristic activities or states. The first is effort or asceticism (*praxis*). This is both positive in cultivating virtue, especially charity, and negative in overcoming the evil thoughts. From asceticism we come to a key Eastern state called *apatheia*. This is not easily translated; it is most certainly not "apathy". There are several words in western spirituality, which point towards the meaning of *apatheia*:

Ignatian "indifference," traditional words like "self-control" or "detachment," the Alcoholic Anonymous "sobriety," or the more modern "spiritual freedom". Its presence or absence can easily be detected when we encounter any of the eight thoughts. They can always attack us, but we manage not to be thrown. We may well feel anger, but we manage a calm or peace, so that we do not become angry. It is not that we are freed from disordered inclinations, but they do not overcome us. We should of course recognise or acknowledge our feelings, even as we can seek to rise above them. We still feel the passions, especially the four principal ones: joy, sorrow, anger and fear. These are not eliminated, but controlled.

Very closely allied to *apatheia* was a later development in Eastern spirituality, *hêsychia* or quiet.[13] It is associated with custody of the heart necessary for contemplation. There is an emphasis on exterior solitude and silence in order to cultivate interior peace. Mere exterior silence is not enough if the heart is dissipated, tugged by attachments, preoccupations and thoughts. We can bring all of these into solitude with us. What is need is vigilance of the heart, using scripture as a weapon against all intrusions. Another word used is "vigilance," which has three levels: careful vocal prayer, meditation and contemplation. Though the word or idea is not found, Eastern theologians see in both the *Institutes of the First Monks* and in the Spanish Carmelite mystics the reality of *hêsychia*.[14]

Hêsychia was no more an end in itself than *apatheia;* it was a way, for some the best way, for union with God. Based on the first stage of *praxis* or asceticism, both look towards the third great goal of the spiritual life that was *theôria* or contemplation. The Eastern tradition is firm: there is no *apatheia* without *praxis,* no *theôria* without *apatheia,* asceticism is necessary to develop serenity or self-control, which is an indispensable condition for contemplation and union with God.

Even with these initial considerations we can approach the chapter of the *Rule* on silence with new eyes. It often struck me that there is very serious weight placed on silence in the *Rule,* far more than might be suggested by the rather legalistic approach we often find – whispering, notes and permissions. "Silence is the cultivation (*cultus* which is literally "worship") of righteousness" (see Is 32:17 in Vulgate) and "in silence and hope will be your strength." These statements about righteousness and strength clearly imply more than keeping our mouths shut.

About a decade ago the Dutch expert on the *Rule,* Kees Waaijman, O Carm, wrote an important article on Carmel's silence.[15] His approach is a careful exegesis of the text in the light of its structure, of its biblical background and of contemporary questions about silence. He is surely right in emphasising the importance of silence for Carmel. But there are insights too from the East in which silence is not the absence of noise or talking, but the cultivation of that inner calm that alone makes contemplation possible. Another dimension will be seen later as we consider Eastern monasticism as illuminating the *Rule.*

Eastern Monasticism

We have already referred to studies that look to Eastern monasticism as a source of insight into our *Rule.* We need not delay either on Albert's stress on the prior and the hermits' relation to him. This matter has been well covered by Mgr Sleiman and Sr Eliane. We might note that the picture of the prior's cell at the entrance to the place reflects what we know elsewhere about Syro-Palestinian monasticism. The monastic laura or lavra, that is a group of cells, had an entrance which was controlled by the prior. Three matters in particular were the concern of the prior: greeting visitors, assigning people who required direction to a trustworthy monk, and deciding on the suitability of those who sought to enter the monastery. There is more involved here than having the prior's cell conveniently near the front door and the phone.

In reading the *Rule* we can usefully keep in mind some features of Eastern monasticism, which are not generally considered by writers on our text. In particular we should look at problems they encountered. The early monks were not generally very literate and they depended on an oral tradition handed down from the elders. One problem was never far from their thoughts: how is it that monks could go astray after many years of fidelity? They knew mental illnesses, such as paranoia, schizophrenia, depression, illusions; they were particularly horrified by suicide, by abandonment of the monastic state and by lapses into extravagances of lust after years of hermit life. All these illnesses and sins they largely ascribed to the work of the devil.

There were three key ways of avoiding such errors, and we find them well developed already in Cassian. The hermit monk was to follow the tradition of the ancients; he should practise humility especially by revealing his state of soul to a reliable spiritual guide; he should exercise moderation.[16] The tradition of the ancients was passed on orally in spiritual direction and also by conferences during which there was discussion, questions and answers. This idea of the community gathering for conferences of course casts a lot of light on the precept about meetings every Sunday (R 15 = 11/13). Likewise, we can sense the urgency of the appeals to humility on the part of the prior and the brothers (R 22-23 = 17-18/19-20).

Elsewhere I have suggested that a key of the Albertine *Rule* is moderation.[17] Not only does it end with a quotation from Cassian, "use discretion (*discretione* not 'common sense') which is the moderator of virtues" (R 24, = Epil./21), but in its brief twenty-four articles it allows exceptions depending on necessity or circumstances over a dozen times. The tradition of discretion, what we would later call "discernment", is a key feature of the *Rule.*

We should also note the Eastern overtones of the two appeals to the "holy fathers" (R 2 and 11 = Prol., 8/2, 9). The appeal to being taught by experience is also a probable reference to the tradition of the holy fathers (R 21 = 16/18). This discretion is found in the presentation of fast and abstinence with their exclusion clauses in cases of necessity.

One of the great problems encountered by the desert fathers was laziness and a related restlessness. Hence we can see the importance of the prohibition against changing cells without permission (R 8 = 5/7) and of the injunction to remain in the cell practising vigilance (R 10 = 7/8). Idleness was obviously a problem on Mount Carmel, hence the very long quotation from Second Thessalonians, one which was frequently quoted in monastic literature. In this Pauline quotation we find the only harsh statement in the whole *Rule*, "whoever is not willing to work should not be allowed to eat either" (2 Thess 3:10 in *Rule* 20 = 15/17). There are several motives adduced for the command to work: idleness exposes us to temptation; work is a service of others; the restless ones (*ambulantes inquiete*) disturb the community.

We have alluded to a constant preoccupation of the monks about why people become unfaithful and defect. The only treatment of this matter is found, surprisingly at first sight, in the article on silence. We are to avoid excessive talking lest we stumble and fall by talking and the fall leads to death (R 20 = 15/17).[18] The author seems to suggest that there is no immediate collapse, but a gradual deterioration of commitment and virtue that can begin as loquaciousness. Failure to observe moderation is a common cause for the collapse of monastic vocation. From Albert we have not only warnings against excessive and unconsidered speech, but also an exhortation to work in silence (R 20 = 15/17), but twice in about fifteen lines he states, "silence is the cultivation of justice" (*cultus iustitiae silentium*, R 21 = 16/18). Justice in the Old Testament – and the text is taken from Is 30:21 – is a sharing in the divine merciful justice and a human imitation of it. In the concrete, justice is the divine gift of salvation and mercy.

Conclusion

We are all familiar with the *Rule* of Albert. An awareness of its Eastern dimensions and echoes allows us to be more alert to further riches. I would not say that it is a purely Eastern creation, but it is one that presents to an alert reader many of the key themes of Eastern spirituality and monasticism.

Notes

1. References to the *Rule* will be by the new (1999) enumeration followed by the traditional O Carm/OCD numbers. Thus art 10 = 7/8, seven being the traditional O Carm number and 8 being the one used in the most recent edition of the Discalced nun's *Constitutions.*
2. E.g. B. Secondin, "What is the Heart of the Rule?" in M. Mulhall, ed., *Albert's Way: The First North American Congress on the Carmelite Rule* (Rome: Carmelite Institute, 1989) 93-132.
3. See C. Cicconetti, *La Regola del Carmelo: Origine-natura-significato* Textus et studia historica Carmelitana 12 (Rome: Carmelite Institute, 1973) 375-385.
4. Cicconetti, *Regola* 376.
5. J. Baudray, "Origines orientales du Carmel? Le mythe et l'histoire," *Carmel* [Venasque] (1974/4) 327-344.
6. On Albert and generally on the *Rule,* see the recent monumental work: V. Mosca, *Alberto Patriarcha di Gerusalemme: Tempo-vita-opere.* Textus et studia historica Carmelitana 20 (Rome: Edizioni Carmelitane, 1996).
7. J. Sleiman, "'Go away from here, Go East' (I K 17:3): Eastern Reflections on the Rule of Carmel" in AA. VV. *The Rule of Carmel.* Conferences on Mount Carmel (Haifa) 4th to 14th October 1999. (Rome: Editrice "Il Calamo," 2000) 93-110.
8. Sr Eliane [Poirot], "La Règle du Carmel et la tradition monastique orientale,"*Carmel* (Venasque 1979) 354-372.
9. Sr Eliane [Poirot], "La Règle du Carmel: Points communs et differences avec le monachisme orthodoxe," *Carmel* (Venasque 1980) 221-231. Both of these articles have been re-published in French with Romanian translations as *Pont entre l'Orient et l'Occident: Règle primitive de l'Ordre de la bienheuruese Vierge Marie du Mont-Carmel* with prefaces by Metropolitan Emilianos Timiadis and Mgr G. Daucourt (Saint-Rémy: Monastère saint Élie-Stânceni: Schitul Sfânta Cruce, 1995).
10. Eliane, "La Règle du Carmel et la tradition" 372.
11. For what follows see T. Spidlík, *The Spirituality of the Christian East: A Systematic Handbook,* Cistercian Studies Series 79 (Kalamazoo: Cistercian Publications, 1986) ch. 9, 233-266.
12. Dorotheos cited Spidlík 233.
13. For overall see T. Spidlík, *La spiritualité de l'orient chrétien: 2. La prière* (Rome: Pont. Instit. Orientale, 1988) ch. 10, "L'hésychasme" 321-356.
14. See J. Besse, "Survivances hésychastes en occident," *Messager orthodoxe* 91 (1982) 7-18 at 12-13.
15. K. Waaijman, "The Silence of Carmel," *Carmelus* 40 (1993) 11-42.
16. J. Cassian, "Conference Two" in C. Luibheid, tr. *John Cassian Conferences.* The Classics of Western Spirituality (New York, Mahwah: Paulist, 1985) 60-80.
17. C. O'Donnell, "Asceticism: Insights from Carmel," *The Way Supplement* 102 (2001) 132-143 at 134-135.

18 . See Waaijman, "The Silence of Carmel" 27-28 and his *The Mystical Space of Carmel: A Commentary on the Carmelite Rule* (Leuven: Peeters, 1999) 222-223.

1. *The Cell*

Sister Teresa Whelan, OCD (Roebuck)

Brothers and Sisters, about this time last year I was asked to speak about the *Rule* at our annual gathering of Carmelite Sisters and in a moment of weakness I agreed. About November I was handed a sheet of paper and I was very excited when I saw the heading – Joint Conference on the Carmelite *Rule.* I thought if I have a chance to attend that I might learn something about the *Rule* that would help me to prepare the talk next August. As I looked down the sheet and saw my name I realised I'd been "conned". Fathers and Brothers, you have all been doing research on the *Rule* to give us Sisters lectures on same, for years and here I am, standing here. I haven't been making any great study in preparation and all I can speak from is my own experience.

When eventually I sat down to think about the eremitical dimension of the *Rule,* the word itself conjured up a very masculine image for me. When I hear the word "eremitical" I see the first hermits on Mount Carmel, you know the picture – the mountain and caves with the hermits in their grey stripped habits. I took out my note book in case I might get some light on the subject and realised I couldn't even spell eremitical. I took out my "page" again and discovered that all three inputs on the eremitical dimension were to be given by women and the community dimension by a man. Community sounds feminine in my ears. Has the Spirit been at work or was it the fairies?

Well before I could go any further I had to have a rethink about the matter and I'm glad to say I now feel perfectly at ease with being eremitical.

Then Our Lady gave me a little nudge and said, "Am I not a hermit?" The *Rule* tells us that we should stay in our cell or nearby pondering the Lord's law day and night. Wasn't it Our Lady that "pondered all these things in her heart"? Yes, for me, Our Lady is the great example of the eremitical life.

Traditionally Carmelites have always had a cell. Do we really need it to be a fixed place, can it not be any quiet place? We can have our favourite spot in the garden or a quiet little hut but given our weather it cannot be permanent. I do believe that we need to have a permanent space, a rock to sit on every day of the year. The same familiar spot, a private space. This is my holy place where I meditate on the law of the Lord day and night. It must be a welcoming place, the place where I meet God. A place of silence and quiet. What happens in this quiet place? I listen. What does God say?

I would like to quote a passage from Cassian I came across in Kees Waaijman's book, *The Mystical Space of Carmel:*

> So we ought to live shut up in our cell. For whenever we have strayed from it and return fresh to it and begin again to live there, we will be upset and disturbed as though we were novice inhabitants. For if we have let it go, we cannot without difficulty and pains recover that fixed purpose of mind which we had gained when we had remained in our cell. Nor is it strange for us who live in a cell, and have our thoughts collected in a very narrow enclosure, to be oppressed by a host of anxieties. The confinement of the cell, which is intended to shape us and gather us up, frightens and oppresses us by its closeness. The only remedy is the persistent will simply to remain in it.

And what he says about monks who are accustomed to work in the open air:

> Whenever they come (to a district where monks are accustomed to work in a cell) they are annoyed by such harassing thoughts and such anxiety of mind that, as if they were beginners and people who had never given the slightest attention to the exercises of solitude, they cannot endure the life of

> the cells and the peace and quietness of them, and are at once driven forth and obliged to leave them, as if they were inexperienced and novices. For they have not learnt to still the motions of the inner person, and to quell the temptests of their thoughts by anxious care and persevering efforts, as, toiling day after day in work in the open air, they are moving about all day long in empty space, not only in the flesh but also in the heart, and pour forth their thoughts openly as the body moves hither and thither.

Maybe Cassian is a bit radical, but what he says about being oppressed by a host of anxieties is, as we all know, quite true.

Isn't the cell the place where I come face to face with myself? Don't I meet all that is within that keeps me from God? At times being in the cell is not easy. I can find plenty of things to keep me justly occupied. It is here that I meet myself in the raw. A great place of purification.

Doesn't prayer involve a deep listening? Edith Stein has said that we need times when we are silent and listen and let the divine Word do its work in us. Isn't the voice of the Lord to be heard in the gentle breeze, therefore we need to be silent within in order to hear it. In silence we confront the untruths and the half-truths. But in silence we also become aware of the healing, loving care of God. Stillness is time to allow oneself to be loved again by God and to accept that love. I was struck by a sentence in the second reading for the feast of St Elijah – St Gregory the Great tells us that wherever we direct our mental gaze, there we may be said to stand.

We might wonder what is the use of the hermit? Is it not true that the more one is anchored in God, the more one is helpful to other people? We have only to look at St Thérèse as she took those steps for a missionary.

It is the second part of the quote from Cassian that really touched me. The monks that work in the fields. I think you all know me well enough to know that if I didn't get out to the fields I'd need medical attention! God gave Adam and Eve the garden of Eden – yes we've fallen from grace but aren't we always striving to re-possess that garden? All our Carmels are blessed with an abundance of nature all around. Mustn't we praise and thank God for this creation by enjoying it? I think what Cassian is referring to is the monks' preoccupation with what they are doing, rather than doing the work but being preoccupied with God. The eremitical dimension of Carmel demands that we do everything else out of our experience of the cell. Referring to Cassian again, it is in the cell that we still the motions of the inner person and quell the tempests of our thoughts.

Reading the Sunday Gospel (Mt 14:13-21) a few weeks ago about the miracle of the loaves and fish I was struck by the words, "where they could be by themselves" and "a lonely place." St Matthew tells us that five thousand men, not counting women and children, were fed and it was still a lonely place. There is a real call for us to be in touch with that lonely place that is within each one of us where God dwells no matter where we are.

The eremitical life of Carmel doesn't just consist in living in the cell. There is a balance of community life, liturgy in common, work, meals in the common refectory. We carry our inner stillness into all aspects of our life and we return to the cell frequently for the refreshment of our stillness.

Life in community helps us to be faithful to the eremitical life. When I was considering religious life I asked the Lord why I just couldn't have a little hut on the mountains and serve him there. The answer came back that to be faithful over time I need the example and "push" from the community.

We are called to live a life of allegiance to Jesus Christ with Mary. We know that Mary lived the village life of Nazareth, so how do I claim that she is a hermit? What happened at the Annunciation? Was Mary sitting pondering the Lord's law? Doesn't pondering include an attentive listening? I think Mary must have been listening very attentively indeed. And what happened when she did hear? She had to keep it all secret in her heart. Who would have believed her? Hearing God's word was more than a joy. What a dilemma! Yes the Annunciation certainly left Mary with a lot to ponder. I believe that it was only her continual pondering over the years on the word of God that helped her to go through the passion, that helped her to help the young church and to be with them. After the resurrection we never hear of her doing anything, just of her being present. Isn't that what we are called to also?

2. *The Nuptial Meaning of the Cell*

Sister Máire Bourke, OCD (Knock)

As an apple tree among the trees of the orchard
so is my Beloved among the young men.
In his longed-for shade I am seated
and his fruit is sweet to my taste.
He has taken me to his banquet hall
and the banner he raises over me is love. *Song of Songs 2:3, 4*

Each of you is to stay in his own cell or nearby,
pondering the Lord's law day and night
and keeping watch at his prayers
unless attending to some other duty. *Rule 7*

Initially, when planning this ten minute input, I intended to take a general approach, to go to the gospels for the passages which showed Jesus going "out to some place where he could be alone and pray" (Lk 5:16), into the hills to be alone and pray to his Father (see Lk 16:12), being led by the Spirit into the desert (see Mt 4:1) and other similar texts, and then to take the "eremitic" texts of the *Rule*, e.g. foundations in solitary places, the separate cells and the prescriptions about the cell, the long number on silence. I suppose I was aiming at an overview, but my mind seemed to keep focusing on the cell – it was like a camera automatically zooming in on the cell. What simple thoughts I have to share then, are clustered around the cell, and they have crystallised in my mind as – *The nuptial meaning of the cell.*

These quotations with which I began are obviously not parallel. But they can complement one another. They are like the fingers of our joined hands, lying alongside each other, interlocking, mutually strengthening and enlightening. I don't intend to compare them, but to isolate three strands from them, and, as it were, plait these strands together. The three strands will be:-

1. The Beloved
2. Desire
3. The Cell

1. *The Beloved:* The *Song of Songs* speaks to the Beloved. From the *Rule* we can identify the Beloved as Jesus Christ, to whom we have chosen to live in allegiance. It is his Word which we ponder. He is the Bridegroom whom we watch for in prayer and through him, the Gate, we enter into the mystery of trinitarian communion – we go freely in and out and are sure of finding pasture.

2. *Desire:* The *Song of Songs* speaks of *"his longed-for shade"*. Longing, desire, is the second strand of the plait – singleness of desire, the pure heart, poverty of spirit where God is the only riches – whatever we call it – I like to call it solitude of desire; and this, to me, is ultimately the meaning of our solitude.

3. *The Cell:* The shade which has been longed-for, the banquet hall; for the Carmelite, a privileged place of encounter with the Beloved. Is the cell the particular treasure of the Carmelite? A good case could be made for it! The eucharist excepted, it is for us the heart of the desert, the heart of the monastery, the heart of the enclosure. For the nuns it is *the* place apart, where no one (thank you St Teresa!), can enter; the place where we "busy ourselves with the Word of God, kneading it into our hearts," to use an expression of St John Chrysostom. (Kneading is a powerful image. Probably most of us here have kneaded bread at one time or another, working with the dough: pushing, pulling, smoothing, turning, caressing it and, if it is yeast bread, leaving it aside in a dark place to rise.) So we knead the Word of God into our hearts, and it purifies them to be capable of receiving the gift of solitude of desire. The cell is the place where we keep watch in prayer; where, in his presence, life's experiences are faced, struggled with, suffered through and where we are fitted to launch out into community. We will be hearing about this cenobitic aspect of the life this afternoon.

The Person of the Beloved, Jesus Christ, solitude of desire and the cell – these are the three strands in my plait. The strength of a plait is in the interweaving and these strands, interwoven, form something very strong, something which is of the essence of Carmel.

Two questions remain for me and this is what came to me about them (you may not agree with me; you may come up with other thoughts):

Can the text of the Rule *itself on the Cell, without help from the* Song of Songs, *support a nuptial meaning?*
Without making any pretence of scholarship, a few things increasingly convince me that it can:

- the importance given to the Cell by nn. 3, 5, 6 and 7

- the intimacy conveyed particularly in n. 3 by "*each* of you ... *separate* cell of *his own* ... I think the Latin conveys it better somehow: *singuli* vestrum *singulas* habeant cellulas *separatas* ... and then of course the whole of n. 7 ...

- the word 'remain' in n. 7. *Maneant*, evoking all the texts in John 15, remain in me; remain in my love; as I ... remain in his (my Father's) love.

- the dialogue with the Lord set up in the cell through pondering his word and watching on him in prayer – this can only be a dialogue of love.

- the spirituality of the medieval Latin hermit which underlies the text. Law follows life and the *Rule* is rooted in the intense love of Christ which characterised the hermit movement of the time.

- the witness to spousal love of e.g. St Teresa and St John the Cross.

What is the relationship between solitude of desire and the cell?
With solitude of desire, the cell, the place of encounter with the Beloved, moves inward to the heart and outward to the "nearby", the monastery, the market place. The spatial cell, physical solitude, hones my desire, and that very solitude of desire, as it

grows, allows my cell (place of encounter) to be everywhere, and at the same time moves me towards my (spatial) cell. So, solitude of desire and the cell are reciprocally formative.

Is the "spatial" cell then a "stage"? Can it be said to have done its work if and when solitude of desire has deepened? In a way, yes; and that is why many people find the Carmelite way helpful. Two strands in their plait are enough. But for Carmel, no; for us the cell is a call, to remain, abide in the cell is a call; to remain attentive and receptive, pouring out love, knowing the gift of God, contemplating the Face of Christ.

In *Nova millennio ineunte* Pope John Paul II speaks of "Gazing on the Face of Christ, the Bride contemplates her treasure and her joy" – and we are all, Mary, the church, ourselves, "the Bride."

3. Remaining in the Cell

Sister Immaculata Glynn, OCD (Hampton)

I have been praying for *apatheia* all morning! Fr Eltin has well said that Sr Máire has said it all – and Sr Teresa said it all, so what is left for me to say? I'm afraid we are going to come down to earth with a bump! I saw my rôle as by way of throwing in a bone to stimulate discussion – when I went to write something down by way of sorting out my ideas, I found I had thrown the bone into my own mind, and then Monday night with Brother Pat Mullins threw in a whole host more of bones and I realised that I was venturing unawares into a minefield! Even describing us as hermits living in community was hazardous - Br Pat would prefer "semi-hermits". In any case the phrase implies the inbuilt – not contradiction – but certainly, tension, in our way of life. So much depends on keeping the balance, but in the very nature of things, the community aspect makes its own demands felt, it is the dominant gene and the scales *are* more inclined to come down on that side, so in order to redress the balance we need to protect and cultivate the eremitical aspect.

I will go back to where I was when the invitation from the Council reached me. We were on retreat – our annual eight day retreat – and for the first time ever we were making it on our own, without a director, and for me anyway, it was a really good experience. Four of us had agreed to take two days each in the kitchen to cover the eight days and I had done my two days early on – I did the necessary minimum for the rest of the time and with no lectures I had long stretches of time in my cell. Among other things I was reading the book on the *Rule: The Mystical Space of Carmel* and was finding it just the right reading for me at the time. Sr Máire's letter arrived into that situation – and I suppose I had never felt more enthused about the eremitical dimension of our life. Because the course was on the *Rule* I picked up that I was being asked to comment on the number that says: "Each of you is to stay in his own cell or near it, meditating day and night on the Law of the Lord and watching in prayer" – so I was really thinking in terms of spending time in the cell. Having just had the experience of having quality time in my cell I was reinforced in my conviction of the importance of getting such time. Then the retreat ended and the business and busyness of life took over again – and I was sort of standing back and watching it happen! Being focused on the idea of the importance of time in one's cell, I became increasingly aware of the need for us to be very strongly convinced that such time *is* important, perhaps more than ever nowadays, because there is so much militating against our getting there, though I do think that time in one's cell has always been a bit of an endangered species. The urgent takes over from the important! I had better speak for myself, but so often if I do get to my cell, I can sit down and immediately things come into my head that I should have done, should be doing, and it takes a very firm conviction that I *should* stay right where I am, meditating on the Law of the Lord, to resist the urge to get up and get busy.

The difficulty is accentuated by the present-day culture, which influences us willy nilly, whether we are aware of it or not and which seems to equate being important with being busy – if you're important you're busy, if you're busy you're important, the primacy of doing over being – whereas our vocation calls us to witness to the opposite scheme of values – the primacy of being over doing. And it takes a strong measure of willpower to give some time to just "sit and be" when you are aware of all the others who are busy doing! All the more so nowadays of course, on account of the dearth of vocations – we are fewer and older, so we have more to do and are probably slower doing it.

Of course, we have to keep the balance – I am not suggesting that anyone should opt out of pulling her weight in the community and of carrying her share of the work load – obedience and charity must always call the tune, and the Lord is to be found in the task of the moment; that is taken as understood. But is it always obedience or charity that keeps me out of my cell? Would it sometimes be more genuine charity to stay in my cell rather than go and see if I could lend a hand elsewhere? I know Holy Mother has plenty to say in the opposite direction. She frequently advised against certain sisters being allowed to have too much time on their own – they needed to be kept occupied. She told M. Maria Bautista that her desire for solitude was in fact much better for her than actual solitude would be. She dismissed the idea that everything depends on our going off into a corner by ourselves and insists that God can and often must be found among the pots and pans. But the pots and pans *do* have a tendency to take over and I find that work has a way of flowing over into all the time there is. So I need to make it my business to have, even at intervals, good stretches of quality time in my cell.

I know my own track record for being in my cell has not been great: I remember, a good many years ago, there were some callers in the afternoon and I couldn't be found – the sister concerned said she had looked for me everywhere. When I said that I had been in my cell all afternoon she said, "Oh I never thought of looking for you there" – which gave me pause for thought! When I used to be working at the altar-breads, which is genuinely very recollected work – I would say very Carmelite kind of work – I used to maintain that being in the solitude there in the baking room was as good as being in my cell. But was it? I see now there is a difference – one big one being that *there* the emphasis was on *doing* rather than in *being.* I remember at the time hearing someone saying how tragic it would be if we as Carmelites were to set our value on the quality and quantity of altar-breads, vestments or cards we produced! Again I was given pause for thought! I have stressed the importance of getting time in our cells and the increasing difficulties of finding that time – and I haven't any real answers to the problem. But where there's a will there's a way and that will – that determination – has to be born of conviction that remaining in our cell is an important, perhaps *the* important, prescription of our *Rule.* The trouble is that that prescription is qualified by "unless attending to some other duty" which could be rendered "if you have nothing better to do!" If we were to think of it in that way –as an optional extra or perhaps a luxury – we wouldn't get there at all.

And when we do get to our cell, what are we doing there? Pondering the Law of the Lord and watching in prayer. That can be hard dry work. We seek him whom our heart loves and we know he *is there* waiting for us, but we often experience his presence as absence. So it is not easy, and certainly no luxury to persevere there in our cell despite the emptiness *and* the restlessness that can take hold of us. But we do know that God *is* there – even in the "nothing".

The book *"The Mystical Space of Carmel"* refers to Mount Carmel as the place or space open to the infinite – transcendent – and compares the cell of the individual hermit to the umbilical cord connecting with that place. Pope Paul VI spoke somewhere of prayer – the continuous prayer of the contemplative – as a subterranean river flowing below the surface of our lives into which we descend at intervals to be renewed and refreshed – I like to think of my cell as having a trapdoor giving access to that river.

So what have I been trying to say? That I believe that getting into our cell for good stretches of time even if only at intervals – on retreat or hermit days – *is* important and that we need to see it as being faithful to the demands of our vocation in its eremitical dimension. Nowadays it is more difficult than ever to find – or make – the time, but where there's a will there's a way if we're sufficiently convinced of its importance.

I think of the parable of the sower – if we put our roots well down into the rich soil of solitude in our cell – alone with the Alone – we will be better able to cope with and survive the thorns and thistles of the cares and busyness of our everyday lives. I am sure that if we honestly do the best we can, God will provide!

1. *The Rule's Relevance for Today*

Liam Finnerty, OCD

A perennial tension

This *Joint Conference on the Carmelite Rule* has been thought-provoking in a number of ways. I should like first to look at the cenobitical dimensions. The opening speaker has already opened up for us the whole panorama of the history of the *Rule* within the context of its ecclesial and magisterial background.[1] But, as a later speaker pointed out, this still leaves us with the unresolved question regarding the tension between the cenobitical and eremitical dimensions of our life.[2] Listening to our Carmelite Sisters in their presentation this morning, I realised the extraordinary way in which the feminine approach can overcome this conflict and reach a more limpid and integrated understanding of the problem.[3]

The conflict between the cenobitical and eremitical aspects of the life are part and parcel of the history of the Order. From Nicholas the Frenchman's *Fiery Arrow* (ca.1270), right down to our own time, this conflict has been present. Merton, in his *Disputed Questions*, examines this problem and concludes that different aspects of the Order's charism have been emphasised at different periods of history.[4] The tension, however, has always made for creativity. It leads to renewal. It has kept the Order on its toes, because at various times these elements needed to be emphasised in one way or another, and the resolutions of the conflict – often intensely felt – have led to renewal at different levels. It could, in fact, be argued that the Reform of St Teresa was itself the result of such a tension. Many aspects of the Reform were indeed very positive but there were negative dimensions as well. It alienated the Ancient Observance from the

Discalced; both began to take up "positions" on various ascetical practices and varying modes of living religious life. It became almost a competition which lacked any inner core of meaning, something quite contrary to the very heart of any religious charism. Such rivalry is now a thing of the past, as this *Conference* clearly testifies and we are discovering together the mutual richness that belongs to the whole family of Carmel.

A fresh awareness of the Rule

At the beginning of everything there is Mount Carmel. It predominates and influences every aspect of Carmelite history and literature. It is extremely beautiful, it is breathtaking. The imagery itself is striking; it elevates the spirit into wholeness and freshness. So the very term "Mount Carmel" itself is elevating, as indeed all spirituality should be. A few years ago I was working with the Social Department in Glasgow with a number of young people who had been expelled from school for serious behavioural problems. There was one particular group which we were trying somehow to reconnect with the educational system. One day, we took them on an excursion to the highlands, to Loch Lomond and Loch Ness. One very difficult young man sat silently all the way there and then, in the afternoon, went off and sat by himself on the rocks. I asked him, "Are you okay? What's wrong?' I will never forget his reply: "I never knew this was my country! I never knew that this could be in Scotland." He had lived all his life in a deprived area of Glasgow and had never experienced nature before in this way. Over the following weeks something new opened up for him, something about "his Scotland". He began to hope that maybe other vistas would open up for him as well, areas unknown in a life that was so broken and deprived. I do not know how well we succeeded in helping him with this discovery, but we certainly tried.

Likewise with the *Rule*. In preparation for this conference I have talked about the *Rule* with many of the friars, around the table in Preston and in other houses as well. Most of us would admit that we had not concentrated enough on the *Rule* over the years, even during our period of formation. One of our directors of formation, now in his eighties, admitted to me that the main focus of formation in his time was the Constitutions. The *Rule,* of course, was important but the principal stress was on the Constitutions. For the friars of the Ancient Observance, on the other hand, I get the impression that the *Rule* was central. My own experience, over the past few weeks in preparation for today, has been one of joy and excitement, as a new awareness and a fresh appreciation of the *Rule* opened up for me. This morning, listening to the Sisters speaking about what the "cell" means, in terms of our Carmelite spirituality and in the context of the overall structure of our life, has also been a moment of light and special insight for me.[5] It has made me reflect, among other things, on my attitude to my own room and the importance I give to it.

Sometimes in the past, I got the impression that the *Rule* was used to imprison, criticise, judge and even disparage any genuine spirit of dialogue and experimentation. Too often the *Rule* (and other aspects of our tradition) has been used in conflict between polarised positions, whether liberal, conservative or whatever. This week has been a new experience of the *Rule* for me – uplifting, inspiring and elevating. An experience of the *Rule* as inspirational in its own right, flowing confidently from its own wellspring of spirituality.

Essential strands

Reflecting on the various elements that make up our Carmelite tradition, we see that the most essential thrust of the *Rule* is the call to live in *allegiance to Jesus Christ;* it is clearly expressed in the opening words. This was something those early hermits and anonymous laymen of the twelfth century understood as a gospel call to follow Christ, a call re-emphasised today in the universal call to holiness as proposed in the documents of Vatican II. They were laymen living their baptismal vows and following the Christian way of life, yet called to something much deeper. In whatever kind of ragbag life they were living they saw the need for intercommunion, for some kind of common identity and cohesion of life. They spontaneously turned to the church, to the then Patriarch of Jerusalem who represented the church in that place. That, in fact, is something highly significant in the cenobitical development of the Order. The approval of Albert is one of the hinge-points through which Carmelite spirituality was to unfold: allegiance to Jesus Christ expressed in the *Rule,* distilled from the living word of God in the scriptures and mediated and confirmed by the historical approval of the church.

The *Rule* thus becomes a living dialogue between *the word of God* and the historical reality of the time in which the word was lived and experienced. And, steeped as it is in the scriptures, the *Rule* links a long tradition from the early monks on Mount Carmel to their spiritual sons and daughters of succeeding generations. Scripture, as we know, is something to be pondered and integrated into our very consciousness and way of thinking. This is the heart of the contemplative element of the *Rule,* its inner core that needs to be embraced in silence and solitude. Without this inner attention, the community dimension itself becomes impoverished and perhaps even meaningless; both sides must complement each other, dovetailing together within the unity of Carmelite spirituality.

So, the first and essential strand of the *Rule* is centred on Christ, and the second must be the place of the scriptures. Thirdly comes the formal incorporation of the Carmelite charism into the *life of the Church.* This last point is significant for, as we have seen, it came from the request of the hermits themselves to be more formally and identifiably part of the church. Albert, for his part, acknowledges this need, addressing them as "brothers, beloved sons in Christ". With this development came canonical recognition and confirmation of a new status and identity. It was also significant spiritually because the community dimension of the charism is thus formally integrated into the life of the church. The final approval of Innocent IV (1247) confirms and protects this status in the *Rule* – celibates living within community.

Thus the Carmelite charism embraces a cohesive whole within the greater reality of the church.

Another major element that must come into consideration is the tradition and culture contained in the writings of the Carmelite authors. These, together with the witness of the Carmelite saints, have allowed for the development of different traditions within *the family of Carmel.* There is a marvellous richness and diversity within the Carmelite family throughout the world, between nuns and friars, and between the different branches of the Order. The writings of the saints contribute hugely to this enrichment, a development to which they themselves are living witnesses. Many commentators have remarked on the link between the first community on Mount Carmel and the early church in Jerusalem, as outlined in the *Acts of the Apostles.* A church in which everyone was equal, brothers and sisters in Christ, and in which goods were held in common – all elements central to the *Rule.* This broad and diverse charism forms part of our identity and has within itself an expansiveness that should not be narrowed down to accommodate any one viewpoint.

Finally, there is *the transformational dimension* of Carmelite spirituality. Without love there is no purpose in our lives; it would be a total waste of time. I am not talking about some kind of esoteric up-in-the-sky love, but a love that is known and experienced in our life together, a love that truly nourishes and leads to spiritual growth. The solitary life, in which transformation of the heart takes place within the cell, needs the complementarity of the community life. Withdrawing into solitude has, for many, meant a crucifixion in a negative sense, not in a creative way. It is not enough to speak of dogmas and doctrines and to tell people to sit quietly in their cell. There is a grave responsibility on all of us, when someone is placed in an eremitical situation, to encourage and support the inner journey. This journey can be experienced as intimidating and destructive, or it can be transforming. For the transformation to take place it needs witnesses, true witnesses to solitude, filled with a spirit of homeliness and hospitality. I know my own heart best, my own "cell", when my outer space has become a place of welcome and hospitality for others. I know myself in a new way when, with true hospitality, I invite the other to share my life. This sharing is in itself transforming for me, so long as it is a hospitality that is real, vital and dependable. Therefore, the solitude in which we place others or ourselves must be surrounded with loving fraternity and sisterhood. Where this does not exist, it is better not to have any such "sharing" at all – no religion is better than bad religion.

Sharing a lived experience

In passing on the tradition, there is a serious responsibility on each of us to discover it, first and foremost, for ourselves, and then to help each other encounter what is at the core of our lives. Before we talk about spiritual intimacy and love as propounded by our saints, we too must have journeyed along some part of that road, and be able truly to share that wisdom with each other. This is paramount for us today, who are growing older, greyer and balder; the challenge must be to open our own hearts in truth and sincerity to those who journey with us. We need to be honest about locating ourselves where we truly are, so that we can walk forward together in our common search, a search that will nourish and sustain us. If we are locked out of our own needs, the grace and power of our charism will never heal the wounds within, and we shall never become sources of life and grace for others. It will then be impossible to create a new springtime in the Order for those who come to share our life.

Notes

1. See Pat Mullins, "General Presentation on the Origins of the Rule" pp. 11-29.
2. This point was made by Eltin Griffin, O Carm who was Facilitator of the *Joint Conference on The Carmelite Rule.*
3. See Sr Teresa, "The Eremitical Dimension of the Rule: 1. The Cell" pp. 86-90; Sr Máire,"The Eremitical Dimension of the Rule: 2. The Nuptial Meaning of the Cell" pp. 91-94; Sr Immaculata, "The Eremitical Dimension of the Rule: 3. Remaining in the Cell" pp. 95-99; Sr Patrice, "The Cenobitical Aspect of the Rule: 2. A journey in Communion to the wellspring" pp. 107-112.
4. Thomas Merton, *Disputed Questions,* (New York: Mentor-Omega Books 1965), pp. 190-6.
5. See note 3.

2. *A Journey in Communion to the wellspring*

Sister Patrice Buckley, OCD (Tallow)

As I pondered on the theme "The cenobitical aspect of the *Rule*", I was drawn to the prayer which we pray daily as communities:

Come Holy Spirit, live in us,
With God the Father and the Son,
And grant us your abundant grace,
To sanctify and make us one.

So it is my experience that it is here, in this communing and in and through the Spirit, in striving to live "a life of allegiance to Jesus Christ" in this sacred space that I am nourished by the Bread of Life at the table, both of the Word of God and the Body of Christ. Here the *Rule* orientates, invites, supports and challenges me to live community. It is his love poured into our hearts by the Spirit which gives birth to, animates our Carmelite communities and forms us as a true family gathered together in his name.

The Journey of the Heart

The *Rule* sets us on a journey, the inward journey, the journey of the heart and orientates the individual journey of the hermit into a communal pilgrimage (see nn. 4, 5, 6). The ascent towards Jerusalem is transposed in terms of interiority, the journey through the Interior Castle, where in the words of Our Holy Mother: "His Majesty has selected the souls he has brought to this monastery", so that the community's deep unity as "a little college of Christ", is centred on our friendship with Jesus. We are called to be "good friends of Jesus and of one another". Carmel is the place, the sacred space, where Teresa saw Christ as the "Living Book" of her cenobitical communities imbued with an eremitical spirit. For Teresa, Albert's *Rule* was not only the juridical nucleus of her Reform, but pre-eminently its spiritual charter. The *Rule,* far from being a juridical code, is a formula for living, for being and becoming that engenders transformation in Christ who leads us to the Fire. Today, I ask: "Does that love within our hearts set fire to others with its flame?"

The First Christian Community

The ideal set forth in the *Rule* is that of a community life which fully reproduces the form and spirit of the First Christian community. The entire text of the *Rule* is imbued with the spirit of comm-union and community. Communion is lived: in silence (18); in solitude (8); in listening love (8); in gathering together for the breaking of the Bread (12); in continuous prayer (8); in dialogue (13); in mutual forgiveness (13); in sharing (10); in spiritual warfare (14, 15, 16); in participating in the common law of work (17); in service (19), where the Word is nourishment for life, unifying our communities and inspiring us to greater fidelity (20). As the hermits assembled together weekly, probably the critical questions were: "Is our community still a sacrament of the reign and presence of God? Is the eucharist still a living and true expression of the breaking and sharing? Yes, we know, community is always on pilgrimage and it disrupts those personal routines and tendencies which draw us towards complacency in any dimension of life.

The Cell

In the *Rule,* the cell is the school of comm-union and community – yes a place of solitude, of keeping vigil, of personal meeting with Jesus through whom in the Spirit, in the depths of our being, we are being fashioned as a sister/brother in relationship. Hence I see the spirituality proposed by the *Rule* at its most profound and challenging level as a spirituality of comm-union, where the eremitical and community dimensions are interwoven to form a mystical tapestry. The *Rule* does not refer principally to isolated persons praying in the cells but rather to a community who are totally committed to a journey in unity, in co-responsibility, singleminded in their dedication to the Lord, united heart and soul, nourished at the table of the Word and the Body of Christ – hermits in community.

To the degree that one has found God in solitude, one mirrors his presence in community: "What we have seen and heard, we are telling you so that you too may be in union with us, as we are in union with the Father and with His Son, Jesus Christ" (1 Jn 1: 3), while St Teresa aptly reminds us that "the holier they are the more sociable they should be with their sisters"; simplicity and joy being fruits of this communion. "From sour faced saints, deliver us, O Lord." Furthermore, it is our experience, if one does have deep bonds in community, one is more likely to experience oneself as personally loved by God which is the only experience that gives meaning to "pondering the Lord's law, day and night". Comm-union is incarnational, so in the cell, the solitary space, relationships are purified, cherished and deepened. Silence is eroded by distance, not by love. True silence is the awareness of the Other and of others with all the dignity and beauty that is theirs. From this milieu, we are challenged to carry one another's burden, we are invited to accept, embrace and foster the giftedness of one another. A spirituality of communion reflected in the *Rule* embraces a spirituality of welcome (7). Silence fosters a manner of relating to my sisters, creating an atmosphere of mutual respect within community, an atmosphere where each one is at home.

The Person of Christ

It is the person of Christ, who gives the Carmelite community its identity – the Word of God is both the person of Christ and the scriptures which offer us Christ – The Message and the Messenger. Christ permeating our life and our living: "Let all you do have the Lord's word for accompaniment" (16). Christ Jesus is not found alone, he is inevitably found within the members of his Body: "A good means to having God is to speak with his friends", and we have Jesus' own words: "where two or three are gathered together in my name, there am I in the midst of them" (Mt 18:20). By his very nature Christ is for others, giving us in the power of his Spirit, the Father's gift of life and love. It is then with his love that we love one another and in that very love we are drawn and bring each other to the experience of deepening communion with him as we see in St John's gospel: Andrew brought Simon to Jesus. Is there any greater gift we can give to one another? As we listen to the anguished cry of the hearts of so many of our people today, in their sense of isolation, loneliness, alienation, how is Carmel bearing witness not only to the transcendence of God, but to his immanence, to comm-union, to friendship, to a sense of belonging, to a fullness of life in communion?

In the *Rule* this journey towards communion is effected when we seek to clothe ourselves in God's armour (16). Here transformation in Christ is not so much an individualistic asceticism, but an ecclesial journey. The highest ideal of community necessarily brings with it conversion from every attitude contrary to communion. Our *Rule* will not allow the individual sister/brother to live according to any personal needs which would have an absolute value. The word "brother" is not used in isolation but in relation to the other members – hence it indicates the relational character of our way of life. The pure in heart shall see God "unswerving in the service of the Lord" (2). This journey is essential, if our words about mutual support, respect, concern, acceptance and accountability are to have any integrity. Here Christ, in his Paschal Mystery remains the source, life-spring, model and measure – "love one another as I have loved you" (Jn 15 :12). We cannot experience true inner freedom unless we strive to live in the truth and suffer the demands of truth, which is what Teresa means by humility. In the *Rule* this journey in evangelical faith, hope and love calls for vigilance. It is a pilgrimage of faith, made in community, guided by the promise of a new Passover, while we live through the trials of a new exodus to be brought to newness in Christ (20, 21).

The Oratory

Finally we see in the *Rule* that pride of place is given to the Oratory (12). Carmel is a community convoked for unity and called each day to drink at the source of love and unity. The power of the Word is at its greatest in the eucharist, which is the foundation of all truth proclaimed and shared and draws us into the life of the Risen Lord. In the *Rule,* eucharist is the new manna which nourishes us in our new exodus. Christ, blessed, broken shared – the mystery of comm-union is celebrated in community. Here Christ is present among us in his Word and in his Body, enlightening our minds, nourishing and firing our hearts – moments of deep communion, of intimacy where we are oned in love. Here our self offering is daily renewed and joined in the self offering of Christ. Here each one comes offering him/herself for comm-union where mutual love is birthed and nourished in the sharing of the one bread, the one cup.

Does this daily celebration renew and fire personal fidelity in communion with The Three, with our sisters/brothers as we strive to reverence the Lord Jesus in our hearts?

Is the sacrifice of Christ, the most important, the most vivifying, the most intimate and personal experience in my life?

Yes we are called to comm-union and we are sent. "Go in peace to love and serve the Lord." The love that unites us is the love that leads us to extend to others the experience of communion with Jesus and with each other. Our communion invites us by its very nature to mission and mission is accomplished in communion. For us today, surely we have seen the heart of this truth brought to its fruition in St Thérèse : "In the heart of my Mother, the church, I will be love." Yes, this *Rule,* this Formula for Living has been enfleshed for us today and for the people of Ireland by St Thérèse – her experience of the person of Christ, the spirituality which inspired her was shared with the world. Her *Story of a Soul* gave us the *Little Way*. In our follow-up to this pilgrimage of grace are we going to bring the sticks together and ignite the fire? "And may that love within our hearts set fire to others with its flame".

The Marian Commentary on the Carmelite Rule By John Baconthorpe (ca.1290-ca.1348)

Christopher O'Donnell, O Carm

With the Baconthorpe commentary on the Carmelite *Rule* we enter a world that may be rather unfamiliar. It is a brief document, a trifle shorter than the *Rule* itself. Our immediate reaction may be to dismiss it as a medieval allegory of no real interest to us, who are sophisticated in our approach to scripture, having little time or respect for interpretations that are not of the kind found in *The New Jerome Biblical Commentary.* That would be a mistake, as all of us are concerned with what Baconthorpe was attempting to do, even though our approach would be different. So we need to suspend our initial reactions and try to be open to a medieval text that at first sight seems superficial and artificial. It is neither. To do this we will need to place Baconthorpe in his era, see what mariology was like in his lifetime, see what the Carmelites were up to, and then we will be in a position to approach the text with more sympathy. I shall end with a few observations from contemporary mariology, leaning mostly on Hans Urs von Balthasar.

John Baconthorpe

We do not have very much detail about the life of John Baconthorpe.[1] His name was John and he was from the village of Baconsthorpe *(sic)* in Norfolk, which is about twenty miles from the great Marian shrine of Walsingham. So one mystery is solved. He was born in the last decades of the 13th century, around 1290. He was provincial of the English province from 1326-1333. In an era in which there were few great theologians, he was one of the best. He was a master of theology at Paris before 1324. He taught there as well as at Oxford and Cambridge.

A contemporary described him as "a man small in stature but great in learning and knowledge." His medieval name was "The Resolute Doctor" (*doctor resolutus*). He wrote a large number of works, many of them lost. They ranged over theology and philosophy; he had a particular interest in canon law. He died in London sometime between 1349 and 1352.

His commentary on the *Rule* was not very accessible even in Latin until the great Staring edition of early Carmelite texts.[2] There is a translation made by Joachim Smet when a student and published in the provincial journal, *The Sword* in 1943.[3] A revised translation is offered at the end of this article.

Mary in the early 14th century

Looking backwards to the Middle Ages we can focus on the great peaks of scholarship, notably Sts Bonaventure and Thomas Aquinas, both of whom died in 1274. In the fifty years or so after their death they would not be at all as revered as they are today. There were many other theologians writing at the time, but even their names are known only to specialists. With regard to Our Lady we can note three currents in writing at the time.[4] The question of the Immaculate Conception was a live issue, and would remain so for more than a century. It had been denied by St Thomas Aquinas but affirmed by the English Franciscan, Duns Scotus (d. 1308). Aquinas could not see how Mary was redeemed in the event of an Immaculate Conception. Scotus saw her as preventatively redeemed, in the same way as St Thérèse thought of a clever doctor removing a stone over which his child might trip. The Carmelites generally followed the Franciscans and were doughty defenders of the doctrine. Though he first denied it, Baconthorpe later became a strong proponent of the Immaculate Conception.

The second topic was theological writings and sermons on the glories of Mary. These were often commentaries on the first part of our *Hail Mary*. There were also many on the Annunciation itself and about events in her life. Thirdly, we find spiritual writing about Mary. These are of various kinds. There were major mystics, like Gertrude of Helfta (d. 1302), Angela da Foligna (d. 1309) and Meister Eckhart (d. 1327) who gave profound intuitions about Mary. There were also prayers composed, especially Psalters of Mary. These were groupings of 150 aspirations or thoughts, which in time would give rise to the rosary. Lastly, there was a growth of lives of Mary, many based on the early third century apocrypha, but with many additions. It was a time of exuberant growth in Marian theology and spirituality.

Carmelite concerns in early 14th century

These were difficult times for the Order. They were newcomers from the Holy Land, arriving between 1230 and 1290. In 1215 the Fourth Lateran Council had prohibited new religious orders. There were various approvals of the Carmelites by popes in succeeding decades, with the problematic striped cloak being changed to white in the reign of Honorius IV at the Chapter of Montpelier in 1287. Lateran IV was reiterated at the Second Council of Lyons in 1274, which allowed some stay of execution for the Carmelites and Augustinians. It was only in 1298 that Boniface VIII gave the requisite papal approval to these latter, by reversing the decree of Lyons. Opposition, however, would last another century.

A key issue was the identity of the Order. We have a preface to the Constitutions of 1281, called the *Rubrica prima,* which claims that Carmelites were authentic followers of an eremitic tradition on Mount Carmel going back to the Prophet Elijah. The successors of these ancient fathers were given a *rule* by Albert in the time of Innocent III. This *First Rubric* may have existed as early as 1247.[5] It was repeated in later constitutions up to 1625. There was a notable addition in the constitutions of 1324, but which may have existed since 1297.[6] The earliest versions of the *First Rubric* sought to answer the question, "When did the Order begin?" The 1324 text poses a further question, "Why are we said to be brothers of the order of blessed Mary of Mount Carmel?"[7]

It adds the following:

> After the Incarnation of Christ their successors built a church in honour of the Blessed Virgin Mary and chose her title, so that afterwards by apostolic privilege they were called Brothers of Blessed Virgin Mary of Mount Carmel.[8]

Though we may smile at vagueness of "after the Incarnation," there is an important point at stake. The editor of early Carmelite texts, Adrian Staring states:

> To be recognised as a religious community in feudal times it was necessary to have a "title," a church or chapel, to the patron of which one placed oneself in service through profession. The *Rule* of St Albert has prescribed an *"oratorium"*. Accounts by pilgrims, 1220-1229, show that the Carmelites had built *"une petite église* de Notre Dame." Thus Our Lady was the patroness of the motherhouse and hence of the whole Order.[9]

We find the title, "Brothers of Our Lady of Mount Carmel" as early as 1252 in papal documents, so it probably already enjoyed popular usage. The leading historian of the Carmelite Order, Joachim Smet, noted, "From these tiny seeds grew the wide spreading tree of the Marian devotion of the Order."[10]

The Elijan-Marian myth

There is one further point to be made before we can approach the commentary of Baconthorpe. The *First Rubric* was developed to furnish a justification for the Carmelite Order going back to Elijah and bringing in the hermits' relationship with the Blessed Virgin in the lst century AD. The first extant text developing the Elijan legend was the chronicle *Universis christifidelibus* dating perhaps from 1289 or the closing years of the 13th century.[11] Soon there would be a linking with Mary in works by contemporaries of Baconthorpe. He himself was perhaps the first to attempt to unite the Elijan and Marian traditions of the Order.[12]

These texts are not history, but they are not unimportant. They belong to what is technically called "myth." A myth is not false, but is a story of origins preserving the values of a society or group. In this sense scholars will refer to Genesis 1-3 as myth:

it is not so much history as theological truth presented in the form of a symbolic narrative. Genesis is not history, but it is nonetheless true. It teaches profound truths such as: God is Creator; all that comes from God is good; men and women are radically equal and both are in the divine image; sin comes from humans; there remains always hope, based on God's promise of redemption.

The Elijan-Marian myth is not history: it does not reflect actual known or verifiable facts about the (uninterrupted!) succession of the prophets and their relations with Mary during her own life in the Holy Land. But it has a truth in the constant inspiration of Elijah and Mary and profound veneration of the Order for them. If you ask why such a myth arose, there are obvious and ready answers.

The myth had the function of compensating for a sense of insecurity and inferiority in the face of the established orders, especially Dominicans and Franciscans. We have already noted the problems for the friars arising from the Councils of Lateran IV and Lyons II. The myth also inserted them into the great traditions of Elijah as the prototype, indeed father, of monks and of the Virgin Mary their chosen patron on Mount Carmel.[13] The myth of succession brings us close to the lived experience of Carmelites as being closely bound to these "founding" figures.

The commentary

The commentary by Baconthorpe begins with a canonical point, one that was crucial in his time, the name of the Order. Every order takes its name from a place or saint. He instances Cistercians from Citeaux and the Black Canons of St Augustine. He then goes on:

> In this manner we are called Brothers of the Order of St Mary in apostolic bulls. We have, indeed, chosen a rule, many points of which the Blessed Virgin observed in her own life.

He then proposes Mary as a model for obedience, poverty and chastity, basing his assertions on the *Rule* and on Luke 1:38, Acts 2:44 and 4:32, Isaiah 7: 14.

He then goes quickly through the *Rule*, making comparisons with Mary for most of the articles. Using phrases like "Likewise the *Rule* states" or "therefore it says in the *Rule*" might at first sight imply that Baconthorpe thinks that Albert, whom he does not name, had Mary in mind when he wrote the *Rule*, but this would be to give too much weight to the comparative words.[14] For his next assertions about Mary, her fasts, her visits to desert places, Baconthorpe relies on one of the many lives or legends about Mary, in this case the *Legenda aurea* of the Dominican Jacob de Voragine (d. 1298), later archbishop of Genoa and the *Scholastic History* of Peter Comestor (the "book-eater", d. ca. 1178).[15]

A parallel for the separate cells is the traditional patristic idea that Mary was alone in contemplation when the angel appeared to her. The common refectory of the *Rule (R 7 = 4/5)*[16] is based on the somewhat banal assumption that Mary ate at home with her parents at Nazareth.

The specification of the common oratory (R 14=10/12) is seen reflected in Mary being in the Temple with other virgins. Baconthorpe gives as his source *De floribus sanctorum*, but the idea is much older, being found in the 2nd/3rd century apocrypha gospel of James (*Protoevangelium*).

There is a significant background to the next part of Baconthorpe's commentary:

> She associated with Joseph from the laity and with John the Evangelist from the higher clergy, each a devout man in his own state of life. In this way she wished our Order to be composed of laity and clerics and in the *Rule* distinguished the hours of devotion of each (cites R 11=8/9).

The Order was originally lay when on Mount Carmel. With Albert it was, as it were, halfway between lay and religious. We know from papal bulls that there were priests from 1229. The Constitutions of London (1281) shows strong clericalisation with a distinction between clerical and lay brothers, with a juridical precedence of the former over the latter. The general chapter at Triers in 1291 deprived the lay brothers of any active or passive voice, a point established in law with the 1324 Constitutions.[17] Baconthorpe is clearly stressing the spiritual identity of both in the Order by stating that both were holy, and implying that both were equally dear to Mary.

Baconthorpe goes on to quote from a spurious letter of Jerome also found in his main source, Jacob de Voragine:

> From morning until the third hour she gave herself to prayer; from the third until the ninth hour she worked at weaving; she did not cease from prayer after the ninth hour until an angel appeared to her bringing her food.

This provides a model for the Carmelite who should pray constantly and work. This regime of the Virgin appears to have come from her "Temple days" as the author had previously indicated her family meals at Nazareth. He draws a further conclusion:

> The fact that she received food from the angel taught us that only simple food is to be taken, which is in keeping with the spiritual life and not meat or wanton food.

This idea of simplicity of food is common in our early literature, being found in John Soreth's commentary on the *Rule*.

Baconthorpe parallels Mary's silence – she spoke only four times in the gospel (Annunciation, Visitation, Finding in the Temple, Cana) – with the prescriptions of the *Rule* (R 21=16/18). He also appeals to Mary's simplicity as he finds in Peter Comestor's *History* that Joseph had brought a cow and an ass to Bethlehem. He deduces, "she rode an ass and not a horse". Means of transport were obviously an issue in Baconthorpe's time too.

By remaining with Jesus when others fled at the passion, Mary showed that she was grounded in great faith, hope and charity. These are to be found emphasised in the *Rule* (R 19= 14/16). Baconthorpe speaks of Mary as a preacher drawing praise, moral instruction and prophecies in her *Magnificat* (see Luke 1:46, 50, 55). Like some of the church fathers Baconthorpe saw in this text evidence of Mary as prophet rather than as preacher.[18]

The parallel in the *Rule* is the injunction, "Let the sword of the Spirit, which is the word of God, dwell abundantly in your mouth and in your hearts" (R 19=14/16). The same *Magnificat* text and Mary's service of Elizabeth gives evidence of Mary's humility and leads to the final articles of the *Rule* which enjoin humility on both brothers and priors (R 22-23=17-18/19-20). He then summarises:

> And since in addition to all the virtues mentioned above, Mary had innumerable others, the *Rule* permits us to go beyond what it proposes. We find in the *Rule:* "If anyone does more, the Lord himself when he comes again will repay him." Finally Mary was discreet in the exercise of all the virtues. We find in the *Rule:* "You are, however, to use discretion, which is the moderator of virtues.' (see R23-24=18, Epil./22-21).

The commentary ends with a paragraph which gives an indication of one reason why it was written, namely in defence of the Order's Marian title:

> Thus it is clear that the Order which has this *Rule,* should have the title "of Blessed Mary". Hence the same Pope Innocent IV who approved the *Rule,* when he gave permission to hear confessions and preach, wrote immediately after: "To my beloved sons the prior general, and provincials of the Order of Blessed Virgin Mary of Mount Carmel health and apostolic blessing." From then until now the Roman Pontiffs in their bulls and letters write the title "of Blessed Mary." Pope John XXII in giving the privilege of exemption bears witness to this when he says: "Your holy Order, planted in the field of the Lord, and specially distinguished with the title of the glorious Virgin Mary, is deservedly honoured by apostolic favours."[19]

That Marian title would be a bone of contention for another half century and would not be resolved before the famous debates between the Carmelite John Hornby and the Dominican John Stokes at Cambridge University in 1374, and about the same time between John of Hildesheim and another detractor, either a

Dominican again or a Franciscan. The disputes concerned the descent of the Order from Elijah and Elisha, its Marian title, the confirmation of the Order and the *Rule,* and the change from a striped mantle to a white one. The university later promulgated a decree affirming the legitimacy of the Marian title, their imitation of, and succession from, the prophets.[20] The matter ended in 1379 when Urban VI granted an indulgence to anybody calling the Order by its Marian title.

Conclusion: The Baconthorpe commentary today

In his polemic John Baconthorpe was anxious to establish that Carmelites lived their *Rule* in imitation of Mary and hence they had a right to their Marian title. One of the key medieval Carmelite Marian themes was just such imitation of their Patroness, Mother and Sister. Imitation as a key norm of true devotion was reiterated at the Second Vatican Council.[21] At the very least John Baconthorpe still invites us to look at our Carmelite life as being in imitation of Mary.

But there is more than thinking of Mary's silence, the *Rule* and our practice. It involves an empathy, and entering into our Carmelite life, with what we prayerfully conceive as the attitude of Mary. It can be seen as living the *Rule* along with Mary, being conscious of what I like to call her "gentle presence".[22]

The Marian theology of Hans Urs von Balthasar points to the fact that Marian spirituality is not just one spirituality among many others, but it is the examplar and foundation of all spiritualities. We grow in discipleship after the example of Mary. In a significant but often overlooked essay written in 1960, he argued that Marian spirituality underlies all others.

> A spirituality centred on the attitude exemplified by Mary, is … not just one spirituality among others. For this reason, although Mary is an individual believer and, as such, the prototype and model of all response in faith, she resolves all particular spiritualities into the one spirituality of the bride of Christ, the church. What we learn from Mary, a lesson for all times, is that the response of the handmaid of the Lord to

> the Word working in her all his will – in such a special and unique manner – is not just one particular theme in theology. What is special in Mary's spirituality is the radical renunciation of any special spirituality other than the overshadowing of the Most High and the indwelling of the divine Word … The idea of making Marian spirituality one among others is, therefore, a distortion …[23]

Today we are invited to do for ourselves what John Baconthorpe attempted in the 14th century. With limited exegetical and historical tools, he sought to bring Mary into the heart of our Carmelite living of the *Rule.* By seeking such integration we can be brought into what Balthasar calls "islands of humanity," which "are those points where people can experience and rediscover authentic realisation and freedom."[24] The Irish theologian, Brendan Leahy, further explains that these islands are:

> Concrete forms of gospel life and mutual love through which Christians would contribute to the rebuilding of a cultural humanism. These are luminous points in the rediscovery of ultimate meaning as revealed in God's movement to us and our moving with him … The "islands of humanity" that von Balthasar proposes can be viewed as expressions of the living prophetic Marian dimension in the church. Since von Balthasar sees Mary as humanity and creation realised, and since there is a continual Marian polarity in the church, we can say that he looks toward the all-embracing principle of the church, with its prophetic, charismatic and mystical dimensions for inspiration and projects to be pursued by the church in the world. The Marian principle points to the primacy of love: love received, responded to, and shared.[25]

Our Marian heritage and our *Rule* point us to a civilisation of love that offers transformation and hope for our world. We are invited to make our contribution in our time, just as John Baconthorpe did in his.

The Commentary on the Rule By John Baconthorpe[26]

A revised translation

The name of every religious order comes from a place or a saint. The Cistercians are named from a place, Cîteaux; so too our Order is from Carmel. Orders are also named from a saint, when his successors choose for themselves his life and rule. Thus the Black Canons are called the Order of St Augustine. In this way we are called "Brothers of the Order of Blessed Mary" in apostolic bulls. We have, indeed, chosen a rule many points of which the Blessed Virgin Mary observed in her own life.

In the first place it is clear that Mary was perfectly obedient, for she said to the angel, "I am the handmaid of the Lord, let it be done for me according to your word." And we find this in the *Rule*: "All the others shall promise him obedience, fulfilling it by deeds."

It is clear that she renounced property. She could not have been outside the apostolic rule, which is called the way of perfection. In Acts 2 we read about this rule: "All who believed were together and they had all things in common;" and later in Acts 5, "And no one said that anything was his own." On this the *Rule* says, "None of the brothers is to claim something as his own; everything is to be held in common."

It is clear that she faithfully observed chastity; it is written of her, "Behold a virgin shall conceive and bear a son." And we find in the *Rule*, "Your loins are to be girded with the belt of chastity."

In the second place the individual chapters are no different. We read that she frequently visited the places where Christ was baptised, where he fasted. These according to the Master [Peter Comestor] in his *History* are desert places and suited for the eremitical life. And since desert and similar places were dear to her, it is said in the *Rule*, "You may take up places in solitary places or in sites given to you" etc.

The saints also agree that when the angel announced the incarnation of the Son of God, he found her in a room apart. And we find in in the *Rule*, "Taking account of the site you propose to occupy, all of you are to have separate cells."

Moreover, she lived in a common place eating and drinking, as at her parents' house in Nazareth. Therefore the *Rule* says, "You are to eat in a common refectory what may have been given to you."

In the book entitled, *Flowers of the Saints,* we read about Mary when she was led to the Temple by her parents, she was not sent off to be alone but with the other virgins in the Temple. Hence the *Rule* adds, "An oratory is to be built in the midst of the cells."

She associated with Joseph from the laity and with John the Evangelist from the higher clergy, each a devout man in his own state of life. In this way she wished our Order to be composed of laity and clerics and in the *Rule* distinguished the hours of devotion of each. Hence it says about clerics, "Those who have learned how to say the canonical hours with the clerics," whilst adding about the laity, "Those who do not know the hours" etc.

Jerome in a letter to Chromatius and Heliodorus said that the Blessed Virgin established a rule for herself: from morning until the third hour she gave herself to prayer; from the third to the ninth hour she worked at weaving; she did not cease from prayer after the ninth hour until an angel appeared bringing her food. Because of her diligence in prayer the *Rule* states: "All are to remain in their cells or near them, meditating day and night on the law of the Lord and being vigilant in prayers." Because of her persistence in work it says: "You should do some work, so that the devil will always find you occupied and he may not through your idleness find some entrance to your souls." Fasting until the ninth hour, she instructed us about fasting. Therefore we read in the *Rule,* "You are to fast every day except Sundays from the Feast of the Exaltation of the Holy Cross etc." The fact that she received foods from an angel taught us that simple food is to be taken which is in keeping with the spiritual life and not meat or wanton food. Hence we find, "You are to abstain from meat, unless it is to be taken as a remedy for illness or weakness," etc.

Mary kept very silent, for do we not read in the gospel that she spoke only four times, as St Bernard notes: to the angel at the Annunciation; to Elizabeth in greeting; at the wedding at Cana; to her Son when she found him? We find in the *Rule* first in general, "The Apostle therefore recommends silence, when he tells us to work in it," etc.; then we find added more particularly, "Therefore we lay down that from the recitation of Compline you are to maintain silence until after Prime the following day."

It is clear that she loved simplicity. When she went to Bethlehem where she gave birth to her Son, we read in the *History* that she brought an ass, not a horse. We find the same simplicity in the *Rule*. "You may have asses or mules" etc.

It is clear that she was firm in great faith, hope and love, when she remained with her Son in his passion, whilst others left him and fled. The *Rule* says about the perfection of love, "Put on the breastplate of justice, so you may love the Lord your God with your whole heart" etc., and "your neighbour" etc. On hope we find, "You may hope for salvation from the one Saviour."

Mary reached the state of preacher. After she had conceived the Son of God, she gave a great sermon, firstly praising God saying, "My soul glorifies the Lord" etc. Then she applied it to his ways: "His mercy is from generation to generation." Thirdly, as a theme of the sermon at the end, she quoted the prophets, "As he spoke to our fathers" etc. Hence we find in the *Rule:* "May the sword of the Spirit which is the Word of God dwell abundantly in your mouths and hearts" etc.

She maintained humility towards God, saying, "Because he looked on the humility of his handmaid,"etc. In the *Rule* subjects are to act this way towards the one in charge, as we find: "you the other brothers are humbly to honour your prior." Mary was humble towards one below her: when she was mother of God, she ministered to the mother of his precursor for three months.

Hence in the *Rule* priors are instructed about humility in these words: "You shall always keep in mind what the Lord said in the gospel, whoever wishes to be greater among you shall be your servant."And since in addition to all the virtues mentioned above, Mary had innumerable others, the *Rule* permits us to go beyond what it proposes. We find in the *Rule:* "If anyone does more, the Lord himself when he comes again will repay him." Finally Mary was discreet in the exercise of all virtues. Hence we find in the *Rule,* "you are, however, to use discretion, which is the moderator of virtues."

Thus it is clear that the Order, which has this *Rule,* should have the title "of Blessed Mary". Hence the same Pope Innocent IV who approved the *Rule,* when he gave permission to hear confessions and preach, wrote immediately after: "To my beloved sons and prior general, and provincials of the Order of Blessed Virgin Mary of Mount Carmel health and apostolic blessing." From then until now the Roman Pontiffs in their bulls and letter write the title "of Blessed Mary". Pope John XXII in giving the privilege of exemption bears witness to this when he says: "Your holy Order, planted in the field of the Lord, and specially distinguished with the title of the glorious Virgin Mary, is deservedly honoured by apostolic favours."

Notes

1. J. *Smet, The Carmelites: A History of the Brothers of Our Lady* of *Mount Carmel*: Vol. 1 Ca. 1200 *until the Council of Trent* (Darien Illinois: Carmelite Spiritual Centre, revised ed. 1988) 50-53, 55; infra Smet, History.
2. A. Staring, ed., *Medieval Carmelite Heritage: Early reflections on the Nature of the Order.* Textus et studia historica carmelitana 16 (Rome: Carmelite Institute, 1989) 193-199. Infra Staring MCH.
3. J. Smet, "Mary Mirrored in our Rule: Commentary on the Rule by John Baconthorpe," *The Sword* 7 (Feb. 1943) 6-11. This has been reprinted in the privately circulated "Early Carmelite Documents. Vol. 1. A Selection for private use by Carmelite Students edited by Richard Copsey" (Rome: Carmelite Institute, 1998) 50-53.
4. L. Gambrel, et al, eds, *Testi mariani del secondo millennio.* Vol. IV *Autori medievali dell'Occidente secoli* XXX-XIV (Rome: Città Nuova Editrice, 1996).
5. See C. Cicconetti, *La regola del Carmelo: Origine, natura significato.*Textus et studia historica carmelitana 12 (Rome: Carmelite Institute 1973) 89-90; see Staring MCH 33-39.
6. Staring, MCH 177.
7. Staring, MCH 41.
8. Staring, MCH 42.

9. Staring, MCH 35.
10. Smet History 8.
11. Staring, MCH 71-90.
12. Staring 178. The work is called *Speculum de institutione* and is in MCH 184-193.
13. See J. Baudry, "Origines orientales du Carmel? Le mythe et l'histoire," *Carmel* (Venasque,1974/4) 327-344 at 340-344.
14. E.g. *"ideo similiter dicitur in regula ... unde dicitur,"* more common is *"et de hoc in regula."*
15. The sources used by Baconthorpe are found in the notes of the critical edition by Staring MCH 193-199.
16. References to the *Rule* are given by the recent agreed numeration of chapters followed by the traditional O Carm chapter and OCD articles from the recent Constitutions of the nuns. Thus R 7=4/5 indicates article 7 in the new numeration, which was chapter 4 in the traditional O Carm scheme and n. 5 in the OCD nuns' Constitutions.
17. See E. Boaga, *Come pietre vive ... per leggere la storiae la vita del Carmelo*. Collana Carmelitana (Rome: Carmelite Institute, 1993) 49.
18. E.g. Origen, *Hom* 8 - PG 13:1819; Jerome, *In Is*. 3:8 - PL 24:115; texts in D. Casigrande, ed., *Enchiridion marianum biblicum et patristicum* (Rome: Ed. Cor Unum, 1974) Nos. 140, 816.
19. The bull of Innocent was 1247 and that of John XXII was 1317.
20. See Staring MCH 326 - 335 with Hildesheim text 336-388.
21. *Constitution on the Church*, LG 66.
22. C. O'Donnell, *A Loving Presence: Mary and Caramel. A Study of the Marian Heritage of the Order*. Horizons 8 (Melbourne: Carmelite Communications, 2000) 95-96; "Core Marian Themes in the Carmelite Order" in J. Welch, ed., *Carmel and Mary: Theology and History of a Devotion* (Washington: Carmelite Institute 2002) 67-68 at 80-84.
23. "Spirituality" in *Word and Redemption. Essays in Theology 2* (New York: Herder and Herder, 1965, from German 1960) 97-98.
24. B. Leahy, *The Marian Profile in the Ecclesiology of Hans Urs von Baltasar* (London-New York-Manila: New City, 2000) 195.
25. Leahy, *The Marian Profile* 195-196.
26. Translated from Latin text of Staring, MCH 193-199.

1. *Lectio Divina*

Introduced by Eltin Griffin, O Carm

1 *Lectio* is a method of Bible reading, which was systematised in the third and fourth centuries.

2 It was very much used by Monastics, East and West.

3 It has come back into general use, ironically via the Missions and through the former Cardinal Archbishop of Milan, Cardinal Carlo Maria Montini. It is one of the great prayer movements in the Church today.

Characteristics of Lectio

4 The Bible text is sacred. Reading the Bible is an experience with God.

5 The text is imaginative and life giving. Unlike the stories we view on TV soaps which often are alienating, the Bible stories can be described as homecoming.

6 We retain the Latin name *Lectio Divina. Lectio* means more than reading. It also means assembling, putting together again.

7 *Lectio* is open to all, educated and less educated even to those whose schooling may have been defective, or who have no literacy skills. *Lectio* brings the Bible back to the people. *Lectio* respects academic study of the scriptures and dismisses fundamentalism.

8 *Lectio* is best described as a dialogue between the Bible and life. Life is reflected in the Bible and the Bible throws light on life.

9 There is a double movement in the Bible as there is in life – sin and grace.

The four moments in Lectio:

1. *Lectio*

Reading slowly, attentively, reverently(aloud) using the current Sunday Gospel in order to be in communion with the whole church savouring the text.

Divide the separate passages.

Feel free to stay with any one section.

A phrase or even a word which strikes one may indicate the way the *Lectio* is to proceed. Absorbing and being absorbed by the text.

2. *Meditatio*

Mulling over

Pondering

God is at work in the world

Where? In our individual lives, in our communities, in the church, in society.

Where do I see the text being fulfilled?

Not "What is the message?"

The two faculties we bring to bear on meditation are memory and imagination. In meditation go deep into the depths of your own life; go wide into the world.

You see the text being fulfilled. Eventually you see the text being universality fulfilled – the wisdom moment.

3. *Oratio*

Happens spontaneously – you feel moved to pray.

The kinds of prayer: Thanksgiving, Repentance, Petition.

Gradually moving into using the words of the text to implant it more fully in one's being.

4. *Contemplatio*

Assimilating the riches received.

Moving into silent communion.
Be open to God's gift of an understanding that goes beyond all sensible understanding.
Read the text again.

Quotations:

Lectio Divina is a walk towards God.
(Mario Masini)

Reading is the foundation of *Lectio Divina*. If you don't read, then the *Lectio* dies.
(Seamus O'Connell)

The poor read the Bible with eyes filled with the faith of the community which tells them: The Bible is God's word. Jesus is alive and present among us. Reading becomes a community activity, a prayerful activity, an act of faith. The poor recreate, with a label and without the name, in a new and updated form, the centuries old practice of the *lectio divina*.
(Carlos Mesters, O Carm)

"I am convinced that for a Christian today, it is difficult, if not impossible, to keep one's faith without nourishing oneself through listening to scripture personally as well as with others. In this way a believer learns to rest in the heart of God and one trains oneself to look at people and their weaknesses with the eyes of God."
(Cardinal Martini)

"Find the heart of God in the Word of God."
(Gregory the Great)

Note: For *Lectio Divina* as in the *Rule* of Carmel, see Carlos Mesters, O Carm: *Meditating Day and Night*, pp 1-7.
(Carmelites, Seapark, Malahide, Co Dublin)

2. *Work in the Carmelite Rule*

Introduced by Christopher O'Donnell, O Carm

One might with some authors wonder about both the place and the space given to work in our short *Rule*.[1] In fact similar questions could be asked about silence. Moreover, the only harshness we find in the whole *Rule* is the peremptory citation from Paul: "If someone is unwilling to work, let him not eat" (2 Thess 3:10). Added to that is the undoubted fact that work is an issue that can lead to quite an amount of friction, lack of charity and anxiety, even in (dare one say especially?) contemplative communities. We need therefore to look carefully at what the *Rule* has to say to us in this matter. The first thing to remark is that our *Rule* is not exceptional in its treatment – parallels can be found in other rules and ascetical treatises from the east to the west. We need to place its teaching in the broad context of the biblical and spiritual traditions.[2] When we do so today, we will realise that we will be dealing with a counter-cultural phenomenon. In our society work is seen often as a necessary evil, a job that allows one to earn money. One's true fulfilment is often what one does apart from work-time. There is a whole gamut of feeling ranging from affirming, disdaining or merely tolerating work. The issue is how we integrate work and spirituality.[3] Unlike the Romans who largely thought that work was for slaves, the Jews had a generally positive approach. God worked in creation for six days. He rested on the seventh (see Gen 1:3-2:3). But six is an imperfect number. The next day is also the continuation of creation by humans who are to have dominion over the earth (Gen1:28-30). Work takes on the character of toil when the relationship with the creator is broken (see Gen 2:17-19, 23). But God did not annul his blessing of the seventh day; the divine precept about rest remained (Gen 2, 3). There are about 500 references to work in the Old Testament. Hard work is praised: it leads to wisdom and allows one to care for the poor (Prov 11:25; 22:9). But the negative view of work as unpleasant is part of the integrity of biblical teaching. The teaching of Jesus abounds in parables which cast work in a positive light, especially agricultural labour (e.g. Mt 21:28-31). He himself was known as a carpenter and a carpenter's son (Mk 6:3; Mt 13:55). Work in the New Testament was seen as having value when as in the case of slaves it is seen to be united with the sufferings of Christ (1 Pet 2:18-24). We are to serve one another (see Mt 23:11), so that what we do for one another is a work done for Jesus himself (see Mt 25:40). The lazy servant in Jesus' parable is reprobated (see Mt 25:26).

A common teaching in the Fathers of the church is the dignity of the worker, who must above all be paid fairly. The paper in this seminar on the eastern dimensions of the *Rule* also indicates the importance given to work. Anthony advises the hermits to be solicitous of three things: the work of your hands, meditation on your psalms and prayer.[4] A similar idea is found in the rule of Colmcille: "three labours in one day – prayers, work, and reading." The Rule of Benedict states: "Idleness is the enemy of the soul. Therefore, the brothers should have specified periods for manual work as well as for prayerful reading."[5]

With that allusion to Benedict we are approaching the Carmelite *Rule* and its teaching on work. Clearly Albert is worried about idleness and its dangers. In this he follows in a long monastic and ascetical tradition. The first thing that we should remember as we study what our Lawgiver teaches is that he did not divide the *Rule* into chapters. The section on the armour of God, the spiritual weapons ends with the words:

> And whatever you have to do, is to be done in the word of the Lord (*quaecumque vobis agenda sunt, in verbo Domini fiant).*

Immediately there follows:

> You should do some work, so that the devil will always find you occupied (*faciendum est vobis aliquid operis, ut semper vos diabolus inveniat occupatos)* and he may not through your idle-

> ness find some entrance to your souls. In this matter you have both the teaching and the example of Blessed Paul the Apostle; Christ spoke through his mouth; he has been set up and given by God as a preacher and teacher of the nations in faith and truth; in following him you cannot go wrong. In work and weariness, he said, we have been with you, working day and night so as not to be a burden to you; it was not as though we had no right, but we wished to give ourselves as a model for imitation. For when we were with you, we gave this precept: whoever is unwilling to work shall not eat. We have heard that there are restless people going around who do nothing. We condemn such people and implore them in the Lord Jesus Christ that working in silence they should earn their bread. This is a good and holy way: follow it (R20=15/17).

Work is therefore part of the defences against evil: by work we prevent the devil "entering into our souls" (*aliquem intrandi aditum ad animas vestras*).[6] As Kees Waaijman notes, "the chapter on work is clearly an extension of the discussion of the armour of God."[7] There is a positive and a negative statement: the devil is to find us busy; we are not to allow him a point of entry to our souls.

Some Key issues

The first issue is what weight or meaning we should give to the words "some work" (*aliquid operis*).[8] One could suggest that it might mean "not too much". But the text from Paul later in the chapter forces us to set aside this minimal interpretation. Paul speaks about labouring in weariness, day and night, so as not to be a burden and he exhorts the Thessalonians to earn their bread (2 Thess 3:7-12). A second possibility is that "some work" might mean work that does not matter too much. There are problems with this interpretation because Albert demands that we be "always occupied" (*ut semper vos diabolus inveniat occuptos*), a quotation from Jerome's letter to the monk Rusticus.[9] Waaijman suggests that the work needs to be taken seriously, otherwise it will not keep the devil at bay.[10] This kind of work will keep people from being restless idlers (*ambulantes inquiete, nihil operantes).*

The second point is Albert's commendation of the example of Paul. The problem for the Thessalonians was that some of them-expected the Parousia any time, so why bother to plant and harvest when the Lord could come anytime? Is not the new time of the Lord a return to paradisiacal life before labour was imposed on humanity? His answer is brief: work! And he proposes his own example. The point here according to Waaijman is not that Paul was always working, but that when his apostolic labours were over, then he turned to serious work in tent making. His apostolic activity was also work. Therefore we are to work when the other necessary things are done.

There is also an implication that may be drawn from the *Rule* that work is for the support of the community: we earn our bread by work, that is, we contribute to our support. Finally, the way of work is not something that takes from our spiritual striving: it is a "good and holy way" on which we are to walk.

Questions

With all this in mind we can now raise questions for our workshop. We can note at the outset the teaching of our saints that, contrary to what outsiders might think, the Carmelite vocation is a combination of Martha and Mary (see Luke 10: 38-42).

1. The attitudes of our saints to work in the light of the *Rule*, e.g. Teresa of Avila.
2. The amount of work that is appropriate.
3. Anxiety caused by work or assigned ministries.
4. The danger of work becoming a minor idol.
5. The situation of those who are ill and infirm and are unable to work – their feelings and the reassurance needed from the more active members of the community.
6. The problem of excessive physical tiredness.
7. The modern problem of stress caused by deadlines for work commissioned or in service of those outside the community.
8. In general the positive contribution of work to physical, psychological and spiritual health.

9. In general the negative influence of some work(s) on physical, psychological or spiritual well-being.

The Discussion

It will help an understanding of the discussion to know that the membership of the repeated workshop on work was almost entirely Carmelite nuns. During the two workshops there was wide agreement about a number of points. It was agreed that work is an essential part of the Carmelite vocation, though the spirit is different from work in the Benedictine traditions. Many spoke about the problems associated with the work today. There are often deadlines; numbers are reduced; there is much more stress. In our communities we find some people dragged down by work; others find themselves dogged by anxiety about tasks and works. We need to remember Paul: "Have no anxiety about anything"(Ph 4:5) and the prayer at each Mass "Protect us from all anxiety." We need to take care when work appears to impinge on prayer and ask where the problem really lies.

An important discussion arose about the reduced numbers and the lessened physical vigour of community members. There can be an identity crisis for those who can no longer work as they formally did. Great sensitivity is needed in this area. Fewer numbers are doing the same or more work. Many no longer have their youthful vigour. Again, young people have very varied approaches to work: some find it problematic even, or especially housework. Others seem to have less difficulty. The same work can make quite different demands on people, for example gardening can be a hobby for one person; it can be a great trial for another.

There was some lively discussion about earlier approaches to work. People spoke about a former insistence on perfection in work. Nowadays we should seek to do things with an appropriate dedication, thus echoing the genial spirit found throughout our *Rule*. An occasional bit of dust on a door frame is not a disaster. On the other hand there is need for proper care where this matters. A problem can arise where there is competitiveness in work. Everyday cooking should not cause stress. It was also agreed that there is a need for balance; like prayer, work too can be an escape. It has, however, a rightful place in our vocation. Communities vary in their ethos and so in their view of work. Work is both a way in which we earn our living and a means of expressing our solidarity with the poor.

Work can also be a valuable path towards self-knowledge. Some spoke of the need for creativity in work and for doing things in new ways. When people say that for Teresa work did not occupy the mind very much, one needs to ask, is this normative? What new kinds of work are appropriate? Some agreed that the topic of work could usefully be addressed in chapter or community discussion. At the end somebody suggested an approach to work: "relaxed but committed".

Notes

1. E.g. Kees Waaijman, *The Mystical Space of Carmel: A Commentary on the Carmelite Rule,* Fiery Arrow 1 (Leuven: Peeters 1999) 198. The commentary on work is 198 -214.
2. See E. C. Sellner, "Work" in M. Downey, ed. *The New Dictionary of Catholic Spirituality* (Collegeville : Liturgical Press, 1993) 1044-1051.
3. Ibid 1044. What follows is drawn largely from this article.
4. Ibid 1048.
5. *Rule of Benedict* 48 :1.
6. *Rule* 20=16/17.
7. *The Mystical Space* 200.
8. Ibid 202-205.
9. *Epist.* 125:11.
10. Ibid 202.

3. Hospitality in the Carmelite Rule

Introduced by Michael McGoldrick, OCD

A striking aspect of the *Rule* is that the only explicit references to hospitality are in the context of receiving hospitality. The brothers are "to eat whatever may have been given"(7). Permission is given to eat foodstuffs that have been cooked with meat while on a journey so "as to avoid giving trouble to your hosts"(17). I think this is significant. When we mention hospitality it is usually in the context of offering it. Most of us are not good at accepting hospitality! We do not like to be dependent on others. Yes, as God's children we are constantly in the situation of accepting hospitality from God more than giving it. Being able to accept hospitality graciously is a deeply Christian quality.

Even if hospitality were not mentioned explicitly, our call to live "in allegiance to Jesus Christ" and to be "unswerving in the service of the Master"(2), would oblige us to hospitality. Jesus, the Master, is the human face of God's hospitality. Living in allegiance to Jesus will involve revealing something of that hospitality to those we meet. Jesus also invites his followers in many different ways to show hospitality. We are repeatedly told that we must love our neighbour as ourselves (Mt 19:19; 22:39; Mk 12:30 etc.). We are given the example of Mary visiting Elizabeth and Elizabeth in turn extending hospitality to her (Lk 1:39-45). We are reminded that what we do to the least of our brothers and sisters we do to Christ (Mt 25:40). Parables like that of the Good Samaritan (Lk 10:29-37) are further examples of our duty to extend hospitality.

Hospitality seems to be implied in the reference to the location of the Prior's cell: "The Prior's cell should stand near the entrance to your property, so that he may be the first to meet those who approach" (9). This would seem to imply that hospitality is an important aspect of the role of Prior.

The hospitality of prayer is central to our *Rule*. We are encouraged to spend our time "pondering on the Lord's law, day and night and keeping watch at prayer"(10). Prayer has always been seen as of benefit to every part of the body of Christ. Our prayer could well be considered our greatest act of hospitality.

The hospitality of sharing God's word seems also to be implied. "The sword of the spirit, the word of God" is to "abound in our hearts"(19). Surely if it abounds in our hearts we will share it naturally with others who visit or whom we visit.

An important way in which we show hospitality is by creating a space of silence for those who come to visit. The *Rule* affirms that "Silence is the way to foster holiness" (21). Many lay people express a need for a break from the busyness and noise of their daily lives. The silence that has always been seen as characteristic of our houses creates a space where they can feel at home and experience some of their much needed silence.

When speaking of work, the *Rule* seems to imply a hospitality of example. St Paul offers himself as an example of "labouring and weary toiling night and day" (20). The injunction to give ourselves to work suggests that we are also to be an example to others in this. These thoughts on hospitality in the *Rule* are intended to invite discussion and further examination. They do not pretend to be exhaustive!

4. *Silence in the Carmelite Rule*

Introduced by Brian McKay, O Carm

The workshop commenced with a 20 minute input from the presenter. The presentation was based on 19 points:

1. Silence in the *Rule* is about the preservation of contemplation.
2. The Bible speaks regularly about the need of silence for attentiveness to the word of God: See the Wisdom literature, the lives of Jesus and Mary etc.
3. Silence detoxifies and defragments.
4. Silence is not absence – but presence to God. It facilitates the practice of *vacare Deo* and leads to *puritas cordis*.
5. Human maturity needs silence. Human maturity is about love and acceptance of self, God and others. It concerns being at ease.
6. Silence reveals one's identity.
7. Silence gives the ability to see and love the world as God sees and loves it, and so should lead to solidarity.
8. Silence is concerned with right relationships and leads us to reality.
9. Silence enables us to be open and to listen. See Marian spirituality.
10. Silent life is full life because it is full of intimacy with God.
11. Silence is about purification.
12. Silence enables us to live in the world while keeping the heart in the desert.
13. Silence allows the other to be other – it is about true love.
14. Silence allows the freedom to be – the person of silence is less likely to be a control freak, a judge, a manipulator etc.
15. Silence is learned in the cell – it is about interior space.

16. Silence is voluntary solitude kept even in the midst of the people.
17. Quote from St Francis de Sales: "to reform a monastery, it is sufficient to regain seriously the observance of silence".
18. Silence can be about neurosis, comfort, isolation, self-centredness.
19. A person of silence should be an all-rounder.

On both days, a rather lively discussion followed revolving around the practical difficulties faced by all religious nowadays. We do, of course, believe in the need for the preservation of silence, but the demands of everyday life can get in the way. We must prioritise in the ongoing tension between the eremitic and cenobitic aspects of our charism. The conclusion drawn was that we *must* preserve silence in our convents and friaries as this is possibly the greatest gift that Carmel has to offer to the contemporary world.

Many people come to us seeking space, refuge, consolation and healing. A quiet experience can achieve far more than many words. People who come to us often comment that, even to enter our grounds from the busy world provides them with an aura of peace. Getting the right balance between prayer and apostolate, between silence and involvement is vital for our mission in the church. Carmel without silence is not Carmel at all. Silence leads us to maturity. Maturity is a gift of God which inspires us to weigh justly the needs of our neighbours and the call to contemplation.

Silence is not merely something external. It is possible for a Carmelite to be silent externally but to be in inner turmoil. Silence of the heart has to be both sought after and received as pure gift from God. This is the lasting type of silence that the world needs today. In this silence, heart can speak to heart. As St Teresa of Avila says, "you have only to find a place where you can be alone and find Jesus present within you."

Our secret is the secret that God is in us. We become aware of that in the land of silence.

5. Spiritual Armour in the Carmelite Rule

Introduced by Philip McParland, OCD

The imagery of spiritual armour may not be very popular today but it was at the time the *Rule* was written. Influenced by the Letter of St Paul to the Ephesians and indeed by the "mission" of the Crusades, it understands the Christian life in terms of a battle against the forces of evil. Armour is used both to defend and to attack. The *Rule* is in no doubt that it is the devil, the person of evil and the cause of evil, whom we must not only defend ourselves against but also fight proactively.

It is perhaps surprising that the *Rule* names only two things explicitly as being the devil's playground: too much talk and idleness. Too much talk can create destructive gossip and lead to a distortion of the truth. It also prevents silence and the experience of solitude which allows us to access and be attentive to the presence of God living and loving within the human heart. Idleness is a form of aimless living. It lacks self-discipline and can give rise to unnecessary temptations. It can also cause unwelcome interference in other people's affairs.

In relation to the spiritual armour itself which we need to successfully fight the devil, the *Rule* presents us with quite a full and comprehensive list: faith, the Word of God, holy meditations, silence, work, fasting, poverty, chastity, obedience and fraternal correction. Each of these virtues and values is an effective means of keeping our lives centred on the Lord and of freeing ourselves from the oppression of evil.

Two in particular, the Word of God and holy meditations, are worth singling out because of the importance given to them elsewhere in the *Rule* (no.7) and also indeed because of the rediscovery of their value today. The scriptures, God's Word, bring us into direct contact with the Living Lord and are a source of personal encounter with Christ. Holy meditations, which is a way of describing the activity of personal prayer, are essential if we are to grow in friendship with Christ or, in the words of Albert himself, if we are to *"live a life of allegiance to Jesus Christ"*.

Even though today we do not tend to refer to the Christian life as a battle to be fought, the reality this model points to is still all too real. There is no doubting the presence of evil in our world. It has many different forms of expression, some as old as the *Rule,* others new and perhaps more subtle. Furthermore, the evil we experience today still comes from the same source, not psychological conditioning or historical circumstances, but the devil himself. Today's Christians need all the helps available if they are to remain faithful to Christ and bring about the kingdom of God in the world. It would be difficult to better those presented in the *Rule* as spiritual armour.

Father, lead us not into temptation, but deliver us from evil.

Final Homily

Brian McKay, O Carm

There is a delightful story told about a Church of Ireland minister who was invited to preach the sermon at an important gathering in St Patrick's Cathedral, Dublin, some years ago. On the day in question, he ascended the pulpit and faced a large congregation which sat back expecting a good twenty minutes worth of wisdom. He turned to that part of the congregation gathered on his left and spoke one word – God; he then faced those in front of him and spoke one word – God; then he gave his attention to those on his right and spoke one word – God. Finally, he threw his eyes over the entire assembly and said "My dear people, go home and think about it." Well the time has come for all of us to go home and think about what we have heard and seen during these days of grace but we must transfer what we have heard from our minds into our hearts and into our daily lives. So what do I carry home with me this day? What are my impressions of these days on the *Rule*?

To live in allegiance to Jesus Christ

It seems quite obvious that what we are about is the daily following of Jesus Christ and it may even seem unnecessary to mention that allegiance, but when we are together as we have been for the last few days, we catch a glimpse of the tremendous fidelity of Carmelites, both Calced and Discalced, who, quietly and unobtrusively, spend their days attempting to do everything out of love for their beloved Saviour and somehow, the dedication and commitment of all gathered here in this holy place cannot but affect the lives of all who experience this love and commitment. I go away from here with a strong sense of the absolute centrality of the Lord Jesus in all that I do and I feel renewed and refreshed to take up again my work in the church for the spread of his good news.

The Carmelite *Rule* is about total self giving to our beloved Lord, and even the witness of this chapel, this house of formation at Dalgan Park, gives me a strong sense of what this commitment is all about.

Generations of young men have gone out of here to preach the good news and many, as the plaques at the back of the church indicate, paid the ultimate price of their lives to spread the gospel. All of this helps me to realise that it is the following of Jesus Christ through the ups and downs of ordinary living that is important. Perhaps, all of us need to reflect regularly on the place of the Lord in our lives.

Community

Our *Rule* emphasises the importance of coming together in the chapel for daily celebration of the eucharist, in the refectory and the chapter meeting. Our lives are all about sharing what we have and what we are with one another. These days have shown quite powerfully what unity there is and can be between O Carms and OCDs, both male and female, and really we are discovering how much we have in common and what we have to share with each other. We are living through difficult times in our country and in the church, and it is true to say that we need each other more than ever before. My impression of the support that we have shown each other during these days is a source of strength and encouragement for the future. We must make it our care and delight to promote and foster all opportunities to make community together. Without strong community support, our lives will be seriously impoverished.

The Individual

Our forebears were hermits who lived their lives listening attentively for the voice of God and our *Rule* has always emphasised the importance of the individual sister or brother and each one's contribution to the common life. During these days, we have witnessed an extraordinary variety of gifts that reside in a very diverse group of individuals – people who have come to Carmel from very different backgrounds and who bring a wealth of life experience. Maybe it is our appreciation of the variety of gifts and our willingness to use these gifts that make us so attractive to the world outside. If you belong to Carmel, who and what you are as an individual greatly influences who and what you are as a group; we cherish what each one has to offer. I leave this holy place with a renewed sense of my own giftedness and its importance for all my sisters and brothers.

Freedom and Joy

I am sure that there are some people who look at us and feel sorry for our restricted lifestyle and who perhaps even pity us. Looking at all the happy faces, hearing the laughter and listening to the telling of the stories, it strikes me afresh how our living of the *Rule* in fact leads to great freedom and joy. We realise that this *Rule* of ours is intended to cause us to flourish and lead us to deep contentment even in times of trial and tragedy. This week we have made it abundantly clear to each other that our way is a way that leads to full life.

Prayer and Silence

We are all very busy people – perhaps far more busy than we would like. This week, we have again stated strongly and powerfully that without our commitment to prayer and silence in our daily lives, there is a great danger that we will lose touch with the very heart of our charism. Our world needs to rediscover the importance of desert/solitude/silence for healthy and wholesome living and the popularity of the workshop on silence is surely an indication that we treasure the time and space spent in quiet vigilance of heart and we offer this experience of silence to a world of noise and dis-ease with the things of God. We affirm that silence is not an optional extra but an integral part of who we are and what we stand for. Without silence, we may close our convents and friaries. I go home recommitted to making time for vigilance of heart or what we often call the *vacare Deo*, literally vacating ourselves for God, something that can only be done in silence and solitude.

The Spiritual Armour

As we mediate on the law of the Lord by day and night, as we peruse holy scripture, as we celebrate the liturgy of the hours together, as we wait at the table of the Lord, as we pray in solitude, we dispose ourselves to receive the armour of God which is given to us as pure gift by God. This week I became very conscious again of our need to be open to this gift which is lavished upon us and manifests itself in the great theological virtues of love or justice, faith and hope. Of course, we must co-operate with God, but really it is all God's work. It is God who clothes us, his beloved daughters and sons. As our great St Thérèse would affirm – all is grace. Yet again I am struck by the fact that hope is the last of the virtues mentioned in the chapter on the spiritual armour and hope is so greatly needed by the world in which we live – another gift of Carmel to our world.

Conclusion

I could go on for quite a bit longer but I must conclude. Really, when all is said and done, our *Rule* is all about love – love of Jesus Christ, love of each other and love of all God's beloved children. It is given to us to open us to the beauty of all creation. Hopefully, we all go away refreshed and recommitted to living the *Rule* to the best of our abilities. I finish with famous and oft repeated words: "This is a good and holy way – walk in it."

The Rule of Albert as approved by Innocent IV (1247)

A revised translation of the Carmelite Rule

Christopher O'Donnell, O Carm

One of the shortest of the great rules is the one originating with St Albert of Jerusalem (d. 1214), who gave the Carmelites a *Way of Life.* His legislation has come down to the Carmelite Order with some modifications sanctioned by Innocent IV in *Quem honorem* (1247), which scholars today see as constituting it as a rule. This *Rule* inspires the whole worldwide Carmelite family.

There are several English translations each with their own features. Some problems face the translator. Many of the terms used by Albert can have a technical or juridical sense in medieval times. For these one can turn to the studies of Carlo Cicconetti and Kees Waaijman.[1]

There are many biblical citations and echoes; most can be easily identified; some are not so sure. One can then either translate Albert's Latin version, or more dubiously look to modern Bible translations from the Hebrew or Greek originals. A revised translation is offered here, which is somewhat more literal than existing translations so that people may be helped to catch the nuances and occasional ambiguities of the original. The translation offered reflects the fact that the *Rule* was written for male hermits on Mount Carmel. Women of the Carmelite Family will perhaps wish to make their own adaptations.

Though the text challenges each translator in matters of style and consistency, there are few interpretive problems.[2] There is, however, a problem of citing the *Rule.* Throughout its history it has been divided into chapters, articles or sections varying from ten to twenty. The traditional O Carm numbers go back to 1586 when John Baptist Caffardi was Prior General. But there are other divisions, for example the translation of B. Edwards or in the English version of the O Carm *Constitutions* (1995). The *Constitutions* of the OCD nuns have a different set of divisions. In 1999 the General Councils of the two branches (O Carm and OCD) came up with a new agreed enumeration. In this revised translation the new numeration is given prominence. But for those who may encounter other numeration in their reading, the traditional O Carm chapters are given as Roman uppercase capitals (I, II, III...) with the ODC nuns' articles in lowercase Roman numerals (i, ii, iii...).

1 [Prol., i] Albert, called by the grace of God to be Patriarch of the Church of Jerusalem, greets his beloved sons in Christ, B., and the other hermits living in obedience to him near the spring on Mount Carmel: salvation in the Lord and the blessing of the Holy Spirit.

2 [Prol., ii] Many times and in different ways the holy Fathers have laid down that everyone – whatever be their state in life or the religious life chosen by them – should live in allegiance to Jesus Christ and serve him zealously with a pure heart and a good conscience.

3 Now then you have come to me seeking a formula of life according to your purpose, which you are to observe in the future.

4 [I, iii] The first thing I lay down is that you have a prior, one of yourselves, chosen by the unanimous consent of all, or of the greater and more mature part. All the others shall promise him obedience fulfilling it by deeds, as well as chastity and the renunciation of property.

5 [II, iv] You can take up places in solitary areas or in sites given to you, ones suitable and convenient for your observance in the judgement of the prior and the brothers.

6 [III, v] Moreover, taking account of the site you propose to occupy, all of you are to have separate cells; these are to be assigned by the prior himself with the agreement of the other brothers or the more mature of them.

7 [IV, vi] You are, however, to eat in a common refectory what may have been given to you, listening together to a reading from holy scripture, if this can conveniently be done.

8 [V, vii] No brother is permitted to change the place assigned to him or exchange with another, unless with the permission of the prior at the time.

9 [VI] The prior's cell shall be near the entrance to the place so that he may first meet those who come to the place and everything afterwards may be done as he wills and decides.

10 [VII, viii] All are to remain in their cells or near them, meditating day and night on the law of the Lord and being vigilant in prayers, unless otherwise lawfully occupied.

11 [VIII, ix] Those who have learned to say the canonical hours with the clerics should do so according to the practice of the holy Fathers and the approved custom of the church. Those who do not know the hours are to say the *Our Father* twenty-five times for the night office – except for Sunday and solemn feasts when this number is doubled, so that the *Our Father* is said fifty times. It is to be said seven times for the morning Lauds and for the other Hours, except for Vespers when it must be said fifteen times.

12 [IX, x] None of the brothers is to claim something as his own; everything is to be in common and is to be distributed to each one by the prior – that is, the brother deputed by him to this office – having regard to the age and needs of each one.

13 [xi] You may have asses or mules according to your needs and some provision of animals or poultry.

14 [X, xii] An oratory is to be built as conveniently as possible in the midst of the cells; you are to gather daily in the morning for Mass, where this is convenient.

15 [XI, xiii] On Sundays, or other days if necessary, you shall

discuss the welfare of the group and the salvation of souls; at this time excesses and faults of the brothers, if such come to light, are to be corrected in the middle way of charity.

16 [XII, xiv] You are to fast every day except Sundays from the feast of the Exaltation of the Cross until Easter Sunday, unless illness or bodily weakness, or other just cause counsels a lifting of the fast, since necessity has no law.

17 [XIII, xv] You are to abstain from meat, unless it is to be taken as a remedy for illness or bodily weakness. Since you must more frequently beg on journeys, in order not to burden your hosts you may eat food cooked with meat outside your own houses. At sea, however, meat may be eaten.

18 [XIV, xvi] Since human life on earth is a trial and all who want to live devotedly in Christ suffer persecution, your enemy the devil prowls about like a roaring lion seeking whom he might devour. You must then with all diligence put on the armour of God so that you may be able to stand up to the ambushes of the enemy.

19 Your loins are to be girded with the belt of chastity; your breast is to be protected by holy thoughts, for the scripture says, holy thoughts will save you. Put on the breastplate of justice, so that you may love the Lord your God from your whole heart, your whole soul and your whole strength, and your neighbour as yourselves. In all things take up the shield of faith, with which you will be able to extinguish all the darts of the evil one; without faith, indeed, it is impossible to please God. The helmet of salvation is to be placed on your head, so that you may hope for salvation from the one Saviour, who saves his people from their sins. The sword of the Spirit, which is the word of God, is to dwell abundantly in your mouths and hearts. So whatever you have to do, is to be done in the word of the Lord.

20 [XV, xvii] You should do some work, so that the devil will

always find you occupied and he may not through your idleness find some entrance to your souls. In this matter you have both the teaching and the example of Blessed Paul the Apostle; Christ spoke through his mouth; he has been set up and given by God as a preacher and teacher of the nations in faith and truth; in following him you cannot go wrong. In work and weariness, he said, we have been with you, working day and night so as not to be a burden to you; it was not as though we had no right, but we wished to give ourselves as a model for imitation. For when we were with you, we gave this precept: whoever is unwilling to work shall not eat. We have heard that there are restless people going around who do nothing. We condemn such people and implore them in the Lord Jesus Christ that working in silence they should earn their bread. This is a good and holy way: follow it.

21 [XVI, xviii] The apostle therefore recommends silence when he tells us to work in it; the prophet too testified that silence is the promotion of justice; and again, in silence and in hope will be your strength. Therefore we lay down that from the recitation of Compline you are to maintain silence until after Prime the following day. At other times, though silence is not to be so strictly observed, you are to be diligent in avoiding much talking, since scripture states and experience likewise teaches, sin is not absent where there is much talking; also he who is careless in speech will experience evil, and the one who uses many words harms his soul. Again the Lord says in the gospel: an account will have to be given on the day of judgement for every vain word. Each of you is to weigh his words and have a proper restraint for his mouth, so that he may not stumble and fall through speech and his fall will be irreparable and fatal. He is with the prophet to guard his ways so that he does not offend through the tongue. Silence, which is the promotion of justice, is to be diligently and carefully observed.

22 [XVII, xix] You, Brother B., and whoever is appointed Prior after you, shall always keep in mind and practice what the Lord said in the gospel: whoever wishes to be greater among you shall be your servant, and whoever wishes to be the first must be your slave.

23 [XVIII, xx] And you too, the other brothers, are humbly to honour your prior, and rather than thinking about him, you are to look to Christ who set him as head over you; he said to the leaders of the church, "Whoever hears you hears me, and whoever despises you despises me." Thus you will not be judged guilty of contempt, but through obedience you will merit the reward of eternal life.

24 [Epil., xxi] I have written these things briefly for you to establish a way of life for you, according to which you are to conduct yourselves. If anyone does more, the Lord himself when he comes again will repay him. You are, however, to use discretion, which is the moderator of virtue.

Notes:

1. C. Ciconnetti, *The Rule of Carmel* (Darien, Ill.: Carmelite Centre, 1984), an abridgement of *La Regola del Carmelo: origine, natura, signiificato* (Rome: Carmelite Institute, 1973); K. Waaijman, *The Mystical Space of Carmel: A Commentary on the Carmelite Rule* (Leuven: Peeters, 1999).
2. There is one however in number thirteen. Later manuscripts added *ad* to the Latin word *nutrimentum* giving the meaning "for nourishment". The most difficult reading is preferred, omitting the *ad*, so what is involved is the provision of animals and poultry.